The Real Story Behind
Two-tiered ERP
Separating the Marketing
from the Usable Strategy

Shaun Snapp

The Real Story Behind Two-tiered ERP: Separating the Marketing from the Usable Strategy

Copyright © 2014 by SCM Focus Press

For information about this title or to order other books and/or electronic media, contact the publisher:
SCM Focus Press
PO Box 29502 #9059
Las Vegas, NV 89126-9502
http://www.scmfocus.com/scmfocuspress
(408) 657-0249

ISBN: 978-1-939731-37-1

Printed in the United States of America

Cover and interior design by: 1106 Design

Contents

CHAPTER 1

Introduction

Primarily this book is about enterprise software solution architecture. Two-tiered ERP suggests that using a different approach to ERP than has been proposed historically will provide advantages to companies. At the time of this book's publication, there is a great deal of focus on the supposed benefits of two-tiered ERP. However, determining if two-tiered ERP is a good approach requires an understanding of the history of ERP, as well as the history and incentives of those who shape the idea of two-tiered ERP. This book follows on the heels of my book *The Real Story Behind ERP: Separating Fiction from Reality,* for which I performed the most in-depth analysis into the history of ERP ever undertaken. I felt that it made sense to apply this research to the analysis of two-tiered ERP, as currently this is one of the most topical questions in the ERP space.[1]

I can say with confidence that many of the dimensions of analysis covered in this book have never been published before in any outlet. This book will place two-tiered ERP within the context of ERP's history, and will arrive at what, to me, is an unassailable—although unrevealed—conclusion that two-tiered ERP represents a crack in the façade of big ERP. I can also guarantee that those who read this book will be in a far better position to not only understand two-tiered ERP, but to reply to those who make proposals regarding two-tiered ERP.

Books and Other Publications on Two-tiered ERP

As of this book's publication, there were **no** other books on the topic of two-tiered ERP, nor has research into two-tiered ERP been published in any journal any-where. Therefore, any claims that would be made by proponents of two-tiered ERP could only be supported by anecdotal evidence (unless studies have been performed outside of academics, of which I was not able to find any evidence). Furthermore, when I investigated the history of ERP marketing since the inception of the ERP market for the book *The Real Story Behind ERP: Separating Fiction from Reality,* a clear pattern emerged: ERP software vendors, along with the major consulting companies, routinely made predictions that were never tested by ERP software vendors or the consulting companies. When these hypotheses were tested through academic research, **none** of them were proven to be true. Some of these ERP software vendor predictions are explained in Chapter 4: "Analyzing (Some of) the Logic Used to Sell ERP."

ERP was one of the most prominent trends in the enterprise software area, yet ERP as a **whole** is the subject of a relatively small number of studies overall.

---

[1] If a more detailed analysis has been performed, I was not able to find it published anywhere.

Therefore, it is unlikely that there will ever be enough studies about two-tiered ERP to be able to say anything definitive about its effectiveness as a strategy.

Before I begin writing any book, I perform a comprehensive literature review. One of my favorite quotations about research is from the highly respected RAND Corporation, a think tank based in Santa Monica, California—a location not far from where I grew up and where I used to walk with my friend when I was in high school—at that time having no idea of the historically significant institution that I would stroll by on my lost surfing weekends. RAND's *Standards for High Quality Research and Analysis* publication makes the following statement regarding how its research references other work.

> *"A high-quality study cannot be done in intellectual isolation: it necessarily builds on and contributes to a body of research and analysis. The relationships between a given study and its predecessors should be rich and explicit. The study team's understanding of past research should be evident in many aspects of its work, from the way in which the problem is formulated and approached to the discussion of the findings and their implications. The team should take particular care to explain the ways in which its study agrees, disagrees, or otherwise differs importantly from previous studies. Failure to demonstrate an understanding of previous research lowers the perceived quality of a study, despite any other good characteristics it may possess."*

There are so many books that promote ERP rather than analyze ERP, that there was little to reference when doing research for this book—this is a "why" book rather than a "how" book. **Books on ERP have a strong tendency to deal in platitudes and unexamined assumptions,** and offer very little new or different information on the topic. The closest I could find to a book that applied some critical thinking to ERP was *Control Your ERP Destiny: Reduce Project Costs, Mitigate Risks, and Design Better Business Solutions*, which is sort of a "tell all" book about the errors of ERP implementations. However, as with almost all ERP books, it concentrates on providing information to companies to help improve their ERP implementations rather than questioning the logical and evidentiary foundation for ERP. However, this book did not cover two-tiered ERP.

My Background and the Book's Focus and Orientation

It's important to talk about my background. I am an author and independent consultant, and I spent my career working in supply chain planning software. My career has provided me with exposure to not only supply chain software, but also to ERP, reporting, middleware and infrastructure software. I, like the rest of the IT industry, tended to accept ERP systems as a standard. ERP systems were the mother ship to which all other applications connected. When I first began working with ERP back in 1997, I was certified in the SAP ERP Sales and Distribution (SD) module. Back then I had no idea what module to specialize in. Some partner at KPMG looked at my supply chain education and two years of consulting experience and put me onto the Materials Management module training track. I found the training so tedious that after a week I transferred into the Sales and Distribution module and became a certified SD consultant. However, SD proved to be just as tedious as materials management. After five or so months doing things like creating and testing sales orders, I left for i2 Technologies, which at that time was a thought leader in supply chain planning. After hearing so much about how ERP was taking over the world, and how great its supply chain functionality was, I was extremely disappointed to find that the functionality contained in SAP ERP was so elementary. For years I specialized in integrating advanced planning systems to SAP ERP, and on nearly every project I had to account for how the systems that I worked with integrated to SAP ERP—sometimes from the data perspective and sometimes from the process perspective. Therefore, over the years I have accumulated a great deal of exposure to ERP systems and to the systems that connect to ERP. I have also worked in a wide variety of roles, from junior configuration consultant to integration lead, to functional lead, solution architect and system analyst, and even occasionally as a project manager. I have written on a wide variety of supply chain software topics, with my first articles appearing in 2003. My areas of interest extend from documenting the configuration of systems to IT strategy.

The Vendors Covered in This Book

The largest ERP vendors in the world are SAP, Oracle, Microsoft, Infor and Epicor. SAP and Oracle are considered Tier 1 ERP vendors, while Microsoft, Infor and

Epicor are considered Tier 2 ERP vendors. However, it gets more confusing from there because while SAP and Oracle are normally referred to as Tier 1, **they also sell lower tiered ERP systems**.

SAP and Oracle's Tier 1 products are called SAP ERP ECC R/3 and Oracle JD Edwards Enterprise One. Throughout this book, unless I specify otherwise, when I refer to these Tier 1 products, I am referring to SAP or Oracle. When I refer to SAP or Oracle's Tier 2 ERP applications, I will call them "SAP Business One" and "Oracle JD Edwards World."

Because I work with SAP software, most of the examples in this book are from SAP. The Tier 1 market is dominated by SAP and Oracle, and many of the statements regarding SAP generalize to Oracle as well as to Tier 2 ERP vendors. In this book I will also discuss a number of vendors that provide some ERP functionality, but which are neither Tier 1 nor Tier 2 and do not follow the business strategies of the major ERP vendors. Additionally, non-ERP vendors are described in this book to illustrate various principles.

How Writing Bias Is Controlled at SCM Focus and SCM Focus Press

Bias is a serious problem in the enterprise software field. Large vendors receive uncritical coverage of their products, and large consulting companies recommend the large vendors that have the resources to hire and pay consultants rather than the vendors with the best software for the client's needs.

At SCM Focus, we have yet to financially benefit from a company's decision to buy an application showcased in print, either in a book or on the SCM Focus website. This may change in the future as SCM Focus grows—but we have been writing with a strong viewpoint for years without coming into any conflicts of interest. SCM Focus has the most stringent rules related to controlling bias and restricting commercial influence of any information provider. These "writing rules" are provided in the link below:

http://www.scmfocus.com/writing-rules/

If other information providers followed these rules, we would be able to learn about software without being required to perform our own research and testing for every topic.

Information about enterprise supply chain planning software can be found on the Internet, but this information is primarily promotional or written at such a high level that none of the important details or limitations of the application are exposed; this is true of books as well. When only one enterprise software application is covered in a book, one will find that the application works perfectly; the application operates as expected and there are no problems during the implementation to bring the application live. This is all quite amazing and quite different from my experience of implementing enterprise software. However, it is very difficult to make a living by providing objective information about enterprise supply chain software, especially as it means being critical at some point. I once remarked to a friend that SCM Focus had very little competition in providing untarnished information on this software category, and he said, "Of course, there is no money in it."

The Approach to the Book

By writing this book, I wanted to help people get exactly the information they need without having to read a lengthy volume. The approach to the book is essentially the same as to my previous books, and in writing this book I followed the same principles.

1. **Be direct and concise.** There is very little theory in this book and the math that I cover is simple. This book is focused on software and for most users and implementers of the software the most important thing to understand is conceptually what the software is doing.

2. **Based on project experience.** Nothing in the book is hypothetical; I have worked with it or tested it on an actual project. My project experience has led to my understanding a number of things that are not covered in typical supply planning books. In this book, I pass on this understanding to you.

The SCM Focus Site

As I am also the author of the SCM Focus site, http://www.scmfocus.com, the site and the book share a number of concepts and graphics. Additionally, this book contains many links to articles on the site, which provide more detail on specific subjects.

Intended Audience

This book should be of interest to anyone who wishes to learn about two-tiered ERP. However, readers who may find this information most valuable are those who need help determining their company's overall enterprise software strategy.

To get the full benefit of this book, some knowledge of ERP is required. For those starting out, I recommend *The Real Story Behind ERP: Separating Fiction from Reality* as it provides the most exhaustive history of ERP currently published.

If you have any questions or comments on this book, please e-mail me at shaunsnapp@scmfocus.com.

Abbreviations

A listing of all abbreviations used throughout the book is provided at the end of the book.

Corrections

Corrections and updates, as well as reader comments, can be viewed in the comment section of this book's web page. Also, if you have comments or questions, please add them to the following link:

http://www.scmfocus.com/scmfocuspress/erp-books/the-real-story-behind-two-tier-erp/

CHAPTER 2

What is Two-tiered ERP?

We begin with the word "tier," which means a hierarchy. Interestingly if you type the word tier into an image search engine or stock photography site, the most commonly returned image is that of a wedding cake.

Other common images are steps, however the image that I found to be the best analogy is the Kuang Si Falls in Laos—because it signifies integration between the different tiers. As we will see further on in the book, intergration between the various ERP tiers is critical to the two tiered ERP method.

The term "two-tiered ERP" has two meanings. The more general definition, which I have taken from Wikipedia, is as follows:

> *"Two-tier ERP software and hardware lets companies run the equivalent of two ERP systems at once: one at the corporate level and one at the division or subsidiary level. For example, a manufacturing company uses an ERP system to manage across the organization. This company uses independent global or regional distribution, production or sales centers, and service providers to support the main company's customers. Each independent center or subsidiary may have their own business model, workflows, and business processes."*

The second definition, which is attributed to Gartner, is very specific. It imposes certain requirements on how two-tiered ERP is employed and defines different types of two-tier ERP implementations.

> *"Two-tier ERP is the use of different ERP systems at two different layers of the organization:* ***One system serves as the global backbone, often for administrative ERP processes such as financials, human resources and procurement, which are able to be harmonized across all divisions as shared services*** *[bold added]. In addition to the global backbone, one or more ERP solutions (or even reconfigured instances of the same system) are used in parts of the organization to support geographical subsidiary needs, usually for smaller operational requirements, such as sales, marketing, field services and local manufacturing."*

According to Gartner, if there is no **master ERP system** to which the other company's ERP systems are integrated, it is a "zero-tier system." Gartner proposes that, in order for a two-tiered solution to meet the definition, it must include an overseeing or master ERP system or some type of integration that connects up the ERP systems. Furthermore, Gartner has the following to say regarding zero-tiered ERP strategies:

> *"A zero-tier approach, where there is no integration between the core (Tier 1) solution and the solution(s) used by subsidiaries (each operating autonomously under its own profit and loss [P&L] rules), is not considered a tiered strategy—it's also usually a mess waiting to happen. Only if some level of financial consolidation or information sharing among systems is present (subsidiary to core, or subsidiary to subsidiary) is it considered tiered."*

Gartner's definition is a bit too rigid for general use; two-tiered ERP is often described simply as using different ERP systems from different software vendors for different parts of the business. Gartner goes on to propose that two-tiered ERP is not a best-of-breed approach where modules from the different ERP systems are mixed and matched.

> *"The term 'two-tier ERP' has been used for several years, although it is also referred to as 'hub and spoke' or 'multi-tier ERP.' It should not be confused with a best-in-class approach. The main difference is that best-of-breed combines modules from various vendors in an overall solution, whereas a two-tier strategy is the combination of full ERP suites on different layers."*

On this I agree; two-tiered ERP does not combine different modules from different ERP systems.

Two-tiered ERP with Integration to a Master ERP System Versus Business Intelligence Integration

Gartner proposes the following architecture to represent two-tiered ERP.

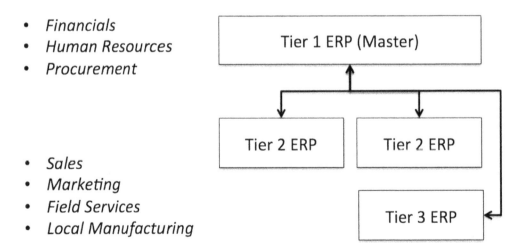

Two Tiered ERP with Master ERP

- *Financials*
- *Human Resources*
- *Procurement*

Tier 1 ERP (Master)

Tier 2 ERP   Tier 2 ERP

- *Sales*
- *Marketing*
- *Field Services*
- *Local Manufacturing*

Tier 3 ERP

Getting ERP systems to integrate to one another is quite a lot of work. If the various companies do not require integration beyond buying and selling from one another, it's unclear why Gartner sees this as preferable. There is little payoff for all the work. Certainly the following architecture is preferable.

Two Tiered ERP with Master BI

- *Financials*
- *Human Resources*
- *Procurement*

Tier 1 ERP (Master)

- *Sales*
- *Marketing*
- *Field Services*
- *Local Manufacturing*

Tier 2 ERP	Tier 2 ERP

Tier 3 ERP

BI(Master)

Companies tend to desire this architecture more as it provides flexibility: different ERP software can be used depending upon the circumstances, but all the ERP systems can be integrated through the business intelligence layer. Gartner seems to consider this to be a two-tiered ERP strategy, as information is shared from the ERP systems.

Actually a software vendor with some of the best material on the topic of integrating multiple ERP systems is Teradata, the well respected business intelligence company. This is explained in one of their white papers.

"The Teradata approach centralizes all legacy data before mapping to the new ERP Environment. This allows significant portions of the migration effort to be reused across multiple source systems. Leveraging existing tools can significantly reduce the time required for data mapping and cleansing tasks.

"The Teradata environment developed during the ERP conversion project provides an alternative to standardizing on a single ERP instance while still enabling a single view of the enterprise. Enterprise-level global visibility can be provided within the Teradata system at a fraction of the cost and time of extending an ERP instance into these regions.

*"Because the road to reducing ERP instances generally stretches across many years, a decision to collapse ERP instances is not taken lightly. Strategic business or cost considerations may dictate that a company looks for alternatives to get to a single view or reduced ERP instances, **but never gets to a single ERP instance** [bold added]. Whatever the case for the company in question, a data warehouse provides the platform that facilitates integration and eases ERP transitions."*[2]

Notice the bolded statement, that while a single instance is often put forward as a goal, that it is often not reached.

Teradata then provides the detail related that comes with moving to a single instance ERP. However, Teradata's applications can also be used to simply manage a two-tiered ERP solution architecture.

---

[2] Lovett, Jeff. Duning, Tim. McDonnell, Monica. *Accelerating the Value of ERP Conversion Projects.* Teradata. 2012.

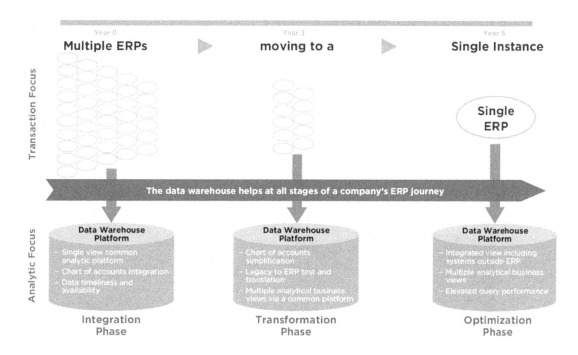

They are speaking here of migrating ERP systems, however, this experience can also be leveraged for integrating multiple ERP systems to a single business intelligence platform. That is with multiple ERP systems integrated to a single business intelligence platform the buyers can receive a comprehensive view of the multiple businesses that are controlled by different ERP systems.

Two-tiered Versus Multi-tiered ERP

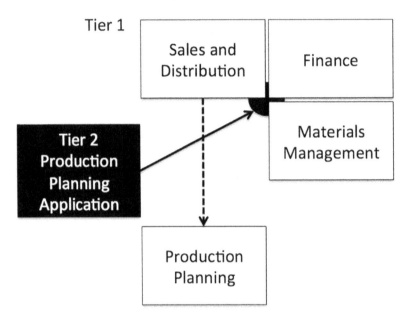

Replacement of Part of ERP With Another ERP

*These last two graphics represent what two-tiered ERP is **not**, which is the integration of different ERP systems.*

Notice that I included a Tier 3 ERP system in the graphic. So while "two-tiered ERP" implies the use of two tiers of ERP systems, in fact, two-tiered ERP can **also mean the use of a third tier ERP system**. Essentially this is another dimension to the definition of two-tiered ERP: two-tiered ERP can mean more than two tiers as explained in the following quotation.

> *"To add to the confusion over terminology, even the second tier, as used in a two-tier strategy, can be misleading. Some companies require more than one additional tier effectively, a multi-tiered*

strategy. Some subsidiaries may require another tiered solution below the second tier, particularly in distribution and retail industries, where an even smaller system may be required to support, for example, franchisees. For the purposes of simplicity, our use of the term 'two-tier ERP' encompasses these multi-tiered solution scenarios, because the strategy determination, governance requirements and selection process are common. In other words, selecting a two-tier approach means that you accept the possibility of a multi-tiered deployment requirement. It's all in the requirements definition."

When one gives the topic some thought, two-tiered ERP is actually a rather strange shorthand for various divisions and subdivisions, as there is also a term called "multi-tier ERP." Multi-tier ERP is where different tier ERP systems—Tier 1, Tier 2 and Tier 3—are deployed, with Tier 3 being used for the smallest of the entities within or associated with the purchasing company. One might propose that "multi-tier ERP" is the more accurate term as it applies more broadly. However, "two-tier" ERP is by far the most commonly used term. As "multi-tier" is used infrequently in practice, I will stick with "two-tier" for this book, and I will use the term "two-tiered ERP" to also **mean multi-tier ERP.**[3]

How Two-tiered ERP Is New

Two-tiered ERP is the opposite of ***single instance ERP***—the long-held logic originally used by ERP software vendors to sell the ERP concept. This logic held that the company should use a single integrated system for all of its subsidiaries. In fact, the reason for the use of the term "tier" is to present the company as a hierarcy of superior and subordinate subsidiaries. However, the term is actually not all that helpful, except to the degree that the higher tier ERP are used for bigger entities and vice versa. Single instance ERP, long held out as a goal by ERP vendors, never became the normal mode of operation. And this is a very important distinction: two-tiered ERP is different conceptually from single instance ERP, but is simply a reflection of what has come to be, and therefore does not differ

---

[3] I will cover the broader implications of this topic in the recommendations section, but there are instances where ERP vendors would be better fits for a two-tiered ERP strategy.

from common practice. This very interesting feature of two-tiered ERP will be discussed in detail in this book, and is central to understanding the concept as well as the reality of ERP.

As has been explained, two-tiered ERP normally means that different types of tiers of vendors are used for different subsidiaries of a company. These tiers correspond to how the ERP vendor is classified. As mentioned in the first chapter, SAP and Oracle are considered Tier 1 ERP vendors, while Microsoft, Infor and Epicor are considered Tier 2 ERP vendors. Generally the systems from Tier 1 ERP vendors have more functionality, are more expensive, and are directed toward the largest companies, as explained by the following Gartner quotation.

> *"Tier 1 vendors that sell ERP systems are typically those that are used by global corporations with annual revenues in excess of $1 billion. Such systems are more complex, provide greater functionality, need higher numbers of trained personnel and have higher cost of ownership. Tier 1 vendors are likely to offer global support to their clients. SAP, Oracle and Microsoft are considered Tier 1 vendors in the ERP space.*[4]

> *"Tier 2 ERP vendors mainly serve mid-market businesses, with revenues from $50 million to $1 billion. Their products are of medium complexity and functionality, and have lower ownership costs than their Tier 1 counterparts. Often they are focused on individual*

---

[4] I disagree with Microsoft being considered a Tier 1 vendor. They have few ERP accounts in the Fortune 1000. Gartner has a financial bias when flattering Microsoft; Gartner takes a great deal of money from Microsoft as is explained in the SCM Focus Press book, *Gartner and the Magic Quadrant: A Guide for Buyers, Vendors, Investors*. Due to this bias, they must show deference to the largest paying software vendors, and Microsoft is a big funder of Gartner. Beyond not being a Tier 1 software vendor, we at Software Decisions analyzed Microsoft's ERP system, Microsoft Dynamics AX, and found it to be one of the lowest scoring ERP systems we have ever reviewed. So Microsoft lacks even a solid Tier 2 ERP system.

industry verticals, whereas Tier 1 products are broad-based. Fujitsu,
Epicor, Ramco and Sage Software are some Tier 2 ERP vendors.

"Tier 3 vendors sell ERP systems that are designed for small
companies that have annual revenues from $10 million to $50 million.
Such systems have the least complexity and costs of ownership; at the
same time, their broader functionality is also much lower. However,
they often have greater focus on individual industry verticals.
Expandable, NetSuite and Syspro are some examples of Tier 3
vendors."

However, this second general definition—or modality of the first definition—is two-tiered philosophy as it is generally implemented. This is expressed in the following quotation:

"A typical set-up is to have Oracle or SAP operating as the primary
system while adding a different tool elsewhere, often using a software-
as-a-service delivery model. Infor, Microsoft, Epicor, Plex, Ultimate
Software, NetSuite, Workday, QAD and IFS are some of the more
frequently used vendors for the secondary deployments, Wang noted."
— Two-tier Strategy a Way to "Reinvigorate" ERP

However, because SAP offers both a Tier 1 and Tier 2 ERP application, a two-tiered strategy could consist of using two different applications from the same software vendor.

If all of this discussion of tiers and ERP applications have left your head spinning, you are not alone. The following graphic should help clarify which vendor is in what tier.

ERP Vendors by Tier

Vendor	Tier 1	Tier 2	Tier 3
SAP	X	X (SAP Business One)	
Oracle	X	X (Netsuite)	X (Netsuite)
Netsuite		X	X
QAD			X
Infor		X	
Microsoft		X	
Epicor		X	
Sage		X	
Rootstock			X
Process Pro			X

*Some view the term "Tier 2 or 3" to be an indicator of software quality or value. **It isn't.** The Tier 1 ERP vendors produce some of the worst-value ERP applications that are sold in the ERP software category. Two of the highest quality and highest value ERP applications that we have evaluated at Software Decisions are actually Tier 2 ERP software vendors.*

To wrap up this chapter, the following features apply to two-tiered ERP:

- Tier 2 ERP software vendors focus on the mid-market, and Tier 3 ERP software vendors focus on the mid-market and even the small market.

- Two-tiered ERP is defined as using applications from different software vendors from each tier. Most often the top tier would use a Tier 1 ERP application (often an on-premises version of the software) while the subsidiaries may use a Tier 2 or Tier 3 ERP application.

- Some Tier 1 ERP vendors recommend using their Tier 1 software for all the various companies. However, this is not a two-tiered strategy; it is a multi-instance strategy—that is a multi-instance of the same application.

Conclusion

The term two tier ERP means applying different ERP systems to different "tiers" of the business. In a nutshell, the larger and more prominent parent companies tend to receive the tier 1 applications, while the subsidiaries receive ERP systems that are considered tier 2. IT analysts and software vendors present a model where multiple ERP systems are connected to a **master ERP system.** There is no real evidence provided as to why this is a good thing, and it is also contradictory to ERP systems, as ERP systems are designed to represent the "enterprise." Furthermore, attempting to integrate multiple ERP systems increases the expense of following a multi-ERP system strategy. There is also no strong delination between the use of the term two tier ERP versus muli-tier ERP strategy. Both refer to the use of multiple ERP systems for various tiers of entities within one business. However, both of these terms are clearly the opposite of the term "single instance ERP," which was an unrealized goal of many buyers that implemented ERP systems, but upon closer examination, there is real justification for the goal of using a single instance ERP system. Certainly using one system can save money as it provides economies of scale—and the more users a single instance of an application has, the lower its costs tend to be per user. However, this relationship cannot be generalized to it being a universally applicable strategy as one must give up flexibility, functionality and must perform more customization to the application as it grows in scope. Complexities in mating one monolithic system to variable requirements was a major reason that the single instance concept, while appealing if one only considered an overly simplistic set of assumptions, never became a commonly implemented approach.

CHAPTER 3

The Reasons for the Rise of Two-tiered ERP

It is important to understand who initially proposed two-tiered ERP, because this tells us a great deal about whose interests it serves.

Two-tiered ERP arose as a marketing strategy specifically by the Tier 2 and Tier 3 ERP software vendors. Its most notable and vocal proponent is the software vendor NetSuite, but now pretty much all ERP vendors, regardless of their tier, have position documents to let prospects and current customers know their preferred strategy.[5] This

---

[5] NetSuite is quite vocal about SAP ERP delivering a poor value, which happens to be well demonstrated by our research at Software Decisions. However, NetSuite is curiously silent on Oracle's value even though Oracle follows a very similar strategy and delivers a similarly poor value. This is easily explained by the fact that NetSuite is owned in part by Oracle and has partnerships with Oracle. Therefore, NetSuite's concern for the value provided by Tier 1 vendors **stops** when it gets to the door of a software vendor that owns a large number of NetSuite shares, who is their partner, and who they rely upon for sales leads. Many do not know that NetSuite and Oracle are joined at the hip, so they may interpret NetSuite's criticism as objective and more effective than if it came from Oracle.

This is the problem with accepting arguments that are based in marketing departments: invariably they are based upon cherry-picked data that is designed to influence by selectively sampling reality.

is the case even though two-tiered ERP is a **direct contradiction** to the single instance logic that Tier 1 vendors have been promoting since the initial development of the ERP software market.

It takes living through the initial ERP sales period in the mid-80s, reviewing the old documentation, or performing interviews to find out that not only was single instance the official proposal of ERP vendors, but that a single instance ERP system would be the **only** system that any ERP customer would ever need to implement. You can now pick yourself up off the floor after falling down laughing, but I kid you not: this was the pitch.

The Background on the Development of the Term "Two-tiered ERP"

Two-tiered ERP was originally conceived of as a philosophical wedge designed to crack open the lucrative Tier 1 ERP market to Tier 2 ERP vendors. The intent of proposing two-tiered ERP was not to present something that was necessarily true, but to sell specific ERP software—and for consulting companies to sell ERP services.

At some point, Tier 1 will be vulnerable to some type of challenge. As is described in part by this book (and in far more detail in, *The Real Story Behind ERP: Separating Fiction from Reality)*, ERP has not achieved the objectives that it was predicted to achieve and many of the ERP systems have aged quite badly. ERP is on its way to being "just another system" instead of the centerpiece of the solution architecture. Overpaying for ERP is now one of the least effective uses of IT budgets. Many large consulting companies misrepresent this fact to their clients. They provide the impression that ERP is so transformational, so important and has such a high ROI that the company should not be concerned with how much they pay for ERP (in particular, how much they pay for their consulting). Nothing could be further from the truth. ERP's often generic functionality, will not improve a business very much, and in order for ERP to have a positive ROI, it must be procured and implemented and maintained **at a reasonable cost**. Two-tiered ERP is an important concept, but not for the reason many people think. It is an important concept because two-tiered ERP represents one of the first cracks in the façade of single instance ERP.

Now, three decades after companies began purchasing ERP systems and preparing themselves for a brave new world of system efficiency, many companies have aging ERP systems as ERP vendors (particularly Tier 1 vendors) are using their ERP systems as **cash cows.** Rather than improving their systems to at least keep them up to date, vendors have used this money to develop new non-ERP applications, which they then attempt to sell into their existing ERP accounts. The applications are not sold on the basis of functionality, usability, or other application-specific factors, but on the idea that the applications will integrate better to their ERP system.

I consult with clients that rely primarily upon ERP systems for supply chain planning, and using these systems is like stepping into a time machine. I was recently working in SAP R/3-ECC-ERP (its name changes depending upon who you are talking to at the time) and was struck by how dated and of poor quality this "flagship" application was in 2013. It has changed very little from the application that I began working with in 1997. And yet, all of that time SAP has been banking support charges that average 20 percent of the initial purchase price **while putting close to nothing back into the product**.

Tier 1 vendors simply have little incentive to continue to develop their ERP systems. Most Tier 1 vendors have saddled their customers with aging and low functionality ERP systems, but with high costs. This is the "ERP trap." Companies that bought big ERP never saw much of a financial benefit, and are now paying an even bigger price as they are stuck with dated systems of low capability that eat up large portions of their IT budget. Every year that I spend time in SAP or Oracle ERP, the more out of date their applications seem.

Is Two-tiered ERP the Savior of ERP?
Generally speaking, the dissatisfaction with ERP systems—and Tier 1 ERP systems in particular—is high. Those that have proposed the concept of two-tiered ERP know this, and have, in part, based their strategy around this dissatisfaction. However, two-tiered ERP is just the latest in a number of popular philosophies that have been proposed to improve and rectify the problems with ERP. The narrative of all these philosophies has never been to question the foundations of ERP (although there is ample evidence to justify doing so), but to suggest a way

of adjusting or improving ERP. What has not been recognized is that many of the criticisms levelled against ERP, and particularly big ERP, are inherent to features of big ERP systems—and therefore not amenable to improvement.

Possibly the most ridiculous of these philosophies was service-oriented architecture (SOA), which was the philosophy prior to two-tiered ERP. Supposedly SOA was going to stoke up the value of ERP systems. At one point all of the Tier 1 and Tier 2 ERP software vendors produced some trumped-up white paper that described their "vision" for SOA. All of the major consulting companies proposed not only that SOA was logical, but predicted that SOA was going to be a **huge trend** that was going to help clients reclaim value from their stogy old ERP systems. Many books were written about this new concept, and many presentations were given at conferences. However, SOA, while proposed with great confidence, has now faded with essentially zero effect on ERP. Interestingly, none of the companies that promised so much from SOA have suffered in the marketplace, and none have had their credibility reduced. Intriguingly, those who pumped up the SOA message are now hoping that recipients of the message have short memories and have by now forgotten about all those SOA promises. It should be stated that the concept of SOA was ludicrous from the beginning, as I explained in the following article that I wrote back in 2010 when SOA was somewhat in vogue.

http://www.scmfocus.com/sapprojectmanagement/2010/07/sap-will-never-support-soa/[6]

The reason SOA was never going to take hold in ERP systems (aside from its technical features; a programmer is better qualified to offer an opinion on that than am I) was because Tier 1 and Tier 2 ERP vendors base their competitive strategy on **closing off options** for their customers—not on publishing their functionality to be used by all. SOA was about breaking down barriers and

---

[6] I was able to find another individual who publicly called out SOA long before it failed, and this was Cynthia Rettig. However, while eventually vindicated (something which I have yet to see anyone point out), at the time she published her article, she was harshly criticized as "too negative" and "not offering real solutions." The following comment on her work at the time is only one example of this criticism.

"There's really nothing new in [Ms. Rettig's] analysis. But Rettig goes a step further and says there's no hope for the future. In fact, while she doesn't offer any remedies for her gloomy prognosis, she does quash one—service-oriented architecture (SOA)."

allowing any application to call upon the functionality of any other application. All Tier 1 and most Tier 2 ERP software is based upon the opposite philosophy: a philosophy of closed-off systems. The ERP system is used as a "wedge" to get into a customer. Once in, the ERP system is used to justify the purchase of uncompetitive applications from the same ERP vendor on the basis of these systems being **easier to integrate back to the ERP system**.[7] Why would big ERP vendors support an approach based on open standards, which would allow their applications' functionality to work flexibly with other applications? That is **exactly the opposite** of their business model. No real technical knowledge was required to predict that SOA would not happen in the ERP space—only knowledge of how big ERP software vendors operate.[8]

Clearly two-tiered ERP is yet another trend to get behind, to write articles about, and to base conference presentations upon. Unlike SOA, it is based upon a number of truths. I want to be clear that the proponents of two-tiered ERP are **not** objective sources of information; they are marketers whose primary motivation is to help sell more software. Two-tiered ERP is a marketing construct based upon a truth (although generally the specific truth is not articulated) that **Tier 1 ERP** systems are not good values for medium-sized companies. In fact, the evidence, which is compiled in, *The Real Story Behind ERP: Separating Fiction from Reality,* is that Tier 1 ERP applications are poor values, even for the largest companies.

A Dangerous Idea

Two-tiered ERP is a threat to Tier 1 ERP vendors because once more diversity is allowed in enterprise software purchases, it will soon be apparent that Tier 1 ERP vendors offer some of the **worst value of all applications** purchased by the enterprise software market. At our companion site Software Decisions, we

---

[7] Research at Software Decisions shows that this single software vendor strategy leaves the buyer with the worst of all worlds: the highest TCO and the lowest functionality, highest implementation risk and lowest ROI.

[8] I had this conversation with a Deloitte consultant back in 2007, where I took the same position I have taken above. At one point he became frustrated with me and said, "I am telling you this is what SAP is saying is the future." At Deloitte, and at the other major consulting companies, one is not supposed to question the "official story." This discipline allows an army of consultants to reliably repeat any message given to them by senior people in the consulting company. Every few years the story changes, often in a way that is inconsistent with earlier official stories. The consultants at the major consulting companies alter their opinions in lock step.

estimated the total cost of ownership (TCO) of purchasing both ERP and non-ERP software from an ERP vendor (a one-hundred-percent ERP vendor software strategy) and the TCO of buying mostly from a Tier 1 ERP vendor. Both strategies are the most expensive purchasing strategies that one can follow, and result in the lowest attainable functionality, implement-ability and usability.[9] Even so, it is still the dominant approach followed by most large and mid-sized companies in the developed countries.

http://www.scmfocus.com/softwaredecisions/plans/solution-architecture-packages/

At Software Decisions, we have performed the background research and believe we are the only entity to publish research on this topic.

Two-Tiered ERP and SaaS

It is widely assumed that "software as a service" (SaaS) is a necessary part of a two-tiered ERP strategy. Two-tiered ERP is about speeding implementation timelines and reducing costs, and both of these objectives are accomplished when using SaaS-delivered solutions.

Matching the ERP System to the Environment

Tier 1 ERP vendors essentially own the Fortune 1000 in the US. Large companies have complex requirements and the IT budgets to match. However, Tier 1 ERP also has a high total cost of ownership, long implementation durations, and a degree of complexity that is a poor match for smaller companies. In fact, a major mistake has been for mid-sized companies to "stretch" to implement Tier 1 ERP. Many of these companies ended up with ERP systems that fell to a low level of capability because the companies lack the funding to support the systems. This is partially because of the software, and partially because ERP software has been parasitized by major consulting companies whose business model is to greatly increase the costs of ERP implementations as well as any other enterprise

---

[9] You can find out about this research at http://www.softwaredecisions.org.

software they implement.[10] I would know, because I have clients that are in this exact predicament. This is truly the worst-case scenario: an expensive system delivering weak functionality and **no real way out**. The ERP system cannot be removed because the company spends so much of its IT budget maintaining the Tier 1 ERP system that they cannot afford to pull out. This is the ERP trap and a vicious cycle. It is a phenomenon that was never considered and never predicted, but is now entirely commonplace.

In these companies, Excel becomes the predominant system for almost all analysis. Everything becomes about extracting data from the ERP system, making changes in Excel, and uploading the output of the processing back to ERP.[11]

Here is an example. One of my clients used a Tier 1 ERP system for forecasting. The forecasting functionality within the ERP system was extremely difficult to use, and was essentially a black box system. The forecast accuracy was abysmal; first, they could not run the forecasting models appropriately, and second, they could not figure out how to interpret the output because the application had no real user interface—data was uploaded and data was downloaded. In truth it was barely an application at all—at least not in terms of how we think of a modern application. Just as big of a problem as the poor output was the time wasted by the employees who had to constantly perform gymnastics to adjust for the poor forecast. For this particular client, I used an inexpensive, but modern, forecasting application to create my own forecasts for the company and to do things they never could have done using the functionality in their ERP system. This is the heavy price that is paid if one relies upon ERP systems for planning functions.

---

[10] A reduction in their profit margin has been a major impediment to major consulting companies recommending SaaS applications, despite the obvious advantages. When Gartner predicted that by 2012, 25 percent of the enterprise software would be delivered by SaaS, they neglected to observe that the major consulting companies would **never be on board** with any approach that reduced their billable hours. As the major consulting companies are very influential in IT decision making, they will slow the movement to SaaS, making any plausible argument to hold on to their highly profitable on-premises consulting business. When the switch does occur, the power will most likely shift from the major consulting companies to the software vendors. This will be a positive development as most consulting companies add extremely little value to IT and primarily are devices for increasing the costs of software implementation, as well as recommending the wrong software to their "clients."

[11] Many companies bemoan the fact that they cannot move away from relying so heavily on Excel, but do not seem to see any correlation to their inability to select and implement good quality software.

Many companies operate as I have just described, and they are operating in a way that is decades behind what is possible. When clients use predominantly Tier 1 ERP systems to get their work done, it saddens me to think of how much human potential is wasted within these companies by working with (and often around) bad software. Poor software selection saddles companies with poor quality applications for many years, and employees are put under pressure to meet objectives that often they cannot meet because the tools they are given are of such low quality. It seems like a bad deal for everyone but a lucky few who benefit from either selling or implementing the software from the major ERP vendors.

The Truth To Two-Tiered ERP

As was discussed previously, two-tiered ERP is based upon an interesting kernel of truth about ERP systems. The actual usage of ERP is explained below:

> *"Our research finds that one-third of companies with more than 1,000 employees use an ERP application supplied by a single vendor while two-thirds use software from two or more vendors; one-third have software from four or more vendors. There are largely two reasons why companies have heterogeneous ERP environments. One is purely historical: Automating back office functions began decades ago, and companies initially did not roll out or upgrade the systems across the entire enterprise. Moreover, some parts of the organization may have been built through acquisitions. If the acquired entity was relatively large, it often made sense to leave the existing systems in place.*

> *"A second reason is that, when it comes to ERP, one size simply does not always fit all; lines of business can be different enough that a single vendor's offering is not well suited to the needs of all. A two-tier approach recognizes that a big ERP system generally, and the headquarters ERP system specifically, often is a bad fit for the needs of a small offsite division or a remote manufacturing unit in, say, Recife, Brazil that is part of a mostly services-oriented corporation. Using the headquarters ERP vendor's manufacturing application capabilities may well be overkill for this single-site operation.*

"Global firms have a long legacy of ERP heterogeneity, with Forrester noting as long ago as 2004 that a third of firms were already running 10 or more instances." — A Strategic Approach to Establishing Two-Tier ERP

Tier 1 ERP vendors would like you to forget that **the vast majority of companies** that use ERP systems **have multiple ERP systems**—sometimes multiple ERP instances in one company—due to things such as each country having its own ERP instance, or a subsidiary in the same country having a separate ERP instance. That is important to consider.

Therefore, part of the two-tiered philosophy is really just "business as usual," although with the rise of the two-tiered philosophy, this is the first time, at least that I could find, that ERP companies diverged from their primary philosophy of a single instance. Tier 1 vendors developed marketing literature on two-tiered ERP after Tier 2 and Tier 3 ERP vendors released their own marketing literature, promoting the use of their applications for all the tiers. This might make for nice marketing literature, and may help muddy the waters, but it makes little sense to simply use a tier 1 ERP system for all business units/subsidiaries, at least if different instances are required (which would be if the different business units/subsidiaries have different configuration and customization needs). Using tier 1 ERP software for all of the tiers undermines the advantages of two-tiered ERP, in that a) the buyer would not receive a diversity of functionality as provided by multiple ERP systems and b) the buyer would not receive any benefits of lowered costs and TCO from lower cost ERP tier 2 and tier 3 ERP systems.

Tier 1 vendors clearly released this marketing literature as a defensive measure—to prevent the Tier 2 and Tier 3 vendors from making much headway with the concept of two-tiered ERP. Customers were reading the two-tiered documentation from smaller ERP software vendors, and wanted to know the position of Tier 1 ERP software vendors (one could have guessed their position before reading their documentation). SAP and Oracle have countered with a second proposal: Continue to use their applications for the second tiers, but use their Tier 2 solutions (SAP Business One and Oracle JD Edwards World). Because these are much less expensive applications. This approach is at least cost effective, but it reduces the competitiveness and diversity of functionality available to the buyer. If a buyer, through a competitive software selection decides to include SAP Business One or Oracle JD Edwards World as their tier 2 ERP system, then that is perfectly fine, but to simply reward these applications with the selection on the basis of the fact that the buyer already owns the vendor's Tier 1 offering makes no sense at all, as there are few technological advantages to doing this.

The Supporting Logic Versus Marketing Hyperbole

Most often two-tiered ERP is presented as something new, but, in fact, it is a very common practice. The real difference is in the acknowledgment that a foundational characteristic—single instance ERP—is giving way to a standard approach of multiple ERP systems, not merely as part of a short-term approach, but as part of a **long-term** strategy. In the past it was considered more appealing to state that, while one had multiple ERP instances, eventually the company would move to a single instance.

The multi-ERP strategy has been around for as long as there have been ERP systems. Yet IT analysts, consulting firms, and IT trade periodicals that discuss the "new trend" of two-tiered ERP strategies, most often fail to bring up the rather important fact that a big part of the ERP value proposition **was supposed to be a single instance of ERP,** as explained in the following quote from an article in the *Sloan Management Review*:

> *"The concept of a single monolithic system failed for many companies.*
> *Different divisions or facilities often made independent purchases,*
> *and other systems were inherited through mergers and acquisitions.*
> *Thus many companies ended up having several instances of the same*
> *ERP system or a variety of different ERP systems altogether, further*
> *complicating their IT landscape. In the end, ERP systems became just*
> *another subset of the legacy systems they were supposed to replace."*

How can so many entities actively promote the concept of two-tiered ERP without even mentioning that it is in complete opposition to one of the original value propositions of buying ERP systems in the first place? This is a good time to analyze just a few of the logics that were used to sell ERP.

Conclusion

At this point two tier ERP comes across to many as a thoughtful enterprise software strategy, however, an analysis of the origins of two tier ERP point to it being nothing more than a marketing construct that was first proposed, or at least popularized by NetSuite. Marketing constructs can be true or false, but it's important to identify the source of any concept in order to understand why it was proposed in the first place. In this case, this construct was designed to open up the clients that were primarily tier 1 ERP customers to tier two and three ERP products. There is really nothing more than anecdotal evidence quoted that is used to demonstrate that two teir ERP systems reduce costs/provide benefits over a 100 percent tier 1 strategy, however, given the high expense and low value of tier 1 ERP systems, it would be surprising if a two tier strategy, if properly configured, did not improve outcomes for buyers. I will explain various two tier ERP strategies and their impact on costs and value in Chapter 6: "Applying the Concept of Two-tiered ERP to Your Company."

Two tier ERP has been co-opted as much as possible by Oracle and SAP, however, at its heart, it is essentially a thinly disguised indictment of tier 1 ERP systems generally, and single instance tier 1 ERP systems in particular. In fact, two tier ERP is one of the first cracks in the façade of tier 1 ERP systems, something that, if enterprise software decisions were primarily based upon research and historical analysis, rather than based upon trends and "what other people are doing," would have occurred some time ago. Another interesting and strange thing about two tier ERP is that while it sounds or seems novel, in fact, it has been the predominant way that companies implement ERP systems—it is only that two tier ERP is explicit in its statement of ERP diversity as a laudable goal—something that was often considered or accepted as simply a transitory state to the "Holy Grail" of a single instance ERP system.

CHAPTER 4

Analyzing (Some of) the Logic Used to Sell ERP

In this chapter we will analyze some of the other logics used to sell ERP systems. These are just the logics that are relevant for the question of two-tiered ERP. A full accounting is made in the book, *The Real Story Behind ERP: Separating Fact from Fiction.* Each one of these logics was important to understanding two-tiered ERP.

One System to Rule Them All: The Single System Logic for ERP

A primary logic used to promote ERP purchases was that the ERP system would be the only system that an enterprise needed to purchase, as explained in the following quotation.

> *"The name is now Enterprise Resource Planning (ERP) systems to suggest that all information systems required for the management of a manufacturing enterprise are part of the solution."* — Process Industry ERP Requirements

When companies that purchased ERP found that ERP did not meet all their business needs, the next idea put forward was to implement the ERP software first, and then to connect non-ERP software (the so-called best-of-breed software) second. This approach is considered desirable because ERP is known as the backbone or the "mother ship," with the other applications connected to it.

The initial idea behind ERP systems was that it would amalgamate many applications into a single system, thus reducing application integration issues. This concept is encapsulated in the quotation below:

> *"Many technical reasons exist including the replacement of disparate systems into a single integrated system."* — Hitt et al., 2002

This turned out never to be the case for the vast majority of companies that implemented ERP software.

> *"The majority of respondents reported that an ERP system fulfills only 30 to 50 percent of IT requirements. As a result, many companies did not abandon their legacy systems but they tend to integrate the functionality from disparate applications."* — ERP and Application Integration: Exploratory Survey

> *"Most pharmaceutical companies have invested in enterprise resource planning systems (ERPs), but few get enough bang for the millions of bucks these platforms cost. It's as if they bought a Lexus loaded with all the extras, but only use it to drive around the neighborhood. 'Most [drug] companies are using ERP for the bare minimum,' says Eric Bloom, vice president of information technology at Endo Pharmaceuticals. To realize the promise of ERPs, pharmaceutical manufacturers must fully integrate them with plant systems such as manufacturing execution systems (MES), quality management systems (QMS), and software for targeted applications such as radio frequency identification, or RFID. For most pharmaceutical companies, the biggest issue is, 'How deep should I take my ERP system into manufacturing?' says Roddy Martin, vice president*

for life sciences industry strategies at AMR Research in Boston."
— Realizing ERP's Untapped Potential

And this is the constant problem: ERP does very little for manufacturing. This is true; in fact, most ERP systems were never really designed with much manufacturing functionality.[12] Often ERP is discussed in terms of its MRP/DRP functionality, but even this is quite basic, not only from a sophistication level, but also from a usability perspective.[13] They can perform basic functions on the inventory level—such as goods issue and goods receipt—but ERP systems cannot be considered as much more than a starter kit for any manufacturing company. Many companies have tried to "get more out of their ERP systems" by pushing them in directions where they were never designed to go (of course, with a healthy dose of customization), but companies that rely on ERP systems in this way cannot hope to properly leverage the available manufacturing software, and will always run their plants at a much lower level of efficiency than companies that adopt the more sophisticated and nuanced IT strategy that is laid out in the book, *Replacing ERP: Breaking the Big ERP Habit with Flexible Applications at a Fraction of the Cost.*

ERP systems never replaced all of the legacy systems in companies that purchased ERP. Therefore, this prediction was spectacularly incorrect. Secondly, ERP vendors did not stick with this principle (of ERP being the only system a company needed to purchase) for very long, as the next section will describe. The fact that they moved away from this logic so quickly makes one wonder if they ever actually believed it themselves.

The Changing Story on ERP's Ability to Meet All Requirements
Soon after the major ERP vendors had saturated the market for ERP software, they began to develop specialized applications for things like supply chain planning, business intelligence, customer relationship management, etc. That is, when the opportunity presented itself, they immediately contradicted their own logic that **they had used to convince so many companies to buy ERP systems.**

---

[12] One of the few exceptions to this is the ERP system ProcessPro. This is an ERP system that is focused on process industry manufacturing. It is profiled in the SCM Focus Press book, *Process Industry Manufacturing Software: ERP, Planning, Recipe, MES & Process Control.*

[13] This topic is covered in detail, along with all of the methods available for both supply and production planning, in the SCM Focus Press book, *Supply Planning with MRP, DRP and APS Software.*

Curiously, a review of the IT/business literature at the time shows that the business/technology press ***did not*** seem to pick up on the fact that this new strategy was at odds with the earlier arguments used to convince companies to buy ERP. I could find no articles that explained how inconsistent the new diversified application strategy was with ERP vendors' own statements made previously.

ERP vendors moved away from providing ERP systems only for several good reasons.

1. *The Single System Approach Was Unworkable:* The single system concept was never anything more than marketing hyperbole—and only a credible hypothesis for the naive, and it is unlikely the vendors actually believed what they were selling. There was simply no way that an ERP system, with its elementary approach to all functionality, could meet all the needs within companies.

2. *Sales Growth:* Once ERP vendors had sold their ERP applications into most of the large and medium to large customers globally, they needed to develop more applications in order to increase their sales. In some cases they could have simply added functionality to ERP; however, this strategy would **not have maximized the ERP vendors' revenues, as they would only get upgrade revenues from their existing clients**. The *trick* was to sell new applications to their existing clients, without having the clients remember that a main justification for purchasing ERP in the first place was that it would cover all of a company's requirements with a single application that contained all of the best practices (more on that later in this chapter). The ERP vendors relied upon both their consulting partners as well as the compliant IT analysts (the ERP vendors being the largest sell-side revenue stream of the major IT analysts) to never point out this minor detail to customers.

Account Control
From the competitive positioning perspective, selling an ERP system to a company was ***one of the best ways ever developed to sell more software (after IBM unbundled software from hardware in 1969)*** into the same company in the future and to control the account. Rather than looking out for the interests

of the buyer, account control is how third parties—such as software vendors and consulting companies—manipulate (or direct, depending upon your preference) their customers into following the interests of the third party. IBM was the first hardware and software vendor to perfect account control and many of their strategies (including how they leased their machines, the prices they charged, the way they dealt with their customers) was based upon account control strategies. Account control is a major force behind how major consulting companies interact with their clients. One example is a "methodology" of software implementation that I once reviewed for Deloitte Consulting as clearly designed around what Deloitte Consulting wanted to sell rather than what made sense from a software implementation perspective. Large consulting companies want more of their own consultants on a project rather than the consultants from the software vendors, because they receive more billing hours and because it helps them control the account and control the information that their customers receive. At large software purchasing companies in particular, the enterprise software market cannot really be understood **without understanding** account control. Unfortunately, that is what many people that work in enterprise software attempt to do.

Once the software vendors had implemented the ERP system at a company, their relationship with that company was based on the fact that they were responsible for that company's largest IT purchase. They had the network effect on their side. The misinformation they passed to their clients reinforced the dubious concept that ERP was somehow the keystone application. They pushed the "boogie man" of integration: that is while the integration from other applications they sold would naturally integrate to their ERP system, the software from other vendors was an "unknown," guarantee that other software from that vendor would integrate to the ERP system at a reasonable cost or in a reasonable timeframe. That was the story anyway; however this was never true.[14]

---

[14] This is repeated by SAP consultants whose opinion seems eerily similar no matter which you speak with. Their opinion is that they would *"prefer to stay"* away from using non SAP applications—because *"they have seen integration issues on previous projects."* Actually, this is not a fact-based opinion—it is a perfect example of financial bias. SAP consultants maximize their income when they simply mirror the viewpoints of SAP itself. This bias is the same as that demonstrated by consulting companies—the "best" software solution for their "clients" is the solution they can make the most money from. If one can predict the advice based upon which selection maximizes the income of the advisor, it is not an objective opinion.

The Boogie Man of Problematic Integration

This integration argument is particularly compelling because the ERP system is considered the central application for a company—the application to which other applications must integrate. This granted ERP software vendors the same type of monopoly power over their customers that Microsoft gained through controlling the operating system on PCs.[15] This monopoly power allowed ERP vendors to unfairly compete by credibly telling their customers that their applications had a head start on integrating to the company's ERP system. In the example of SAP and Oracle, the integration benefits were far more illusory. It's important to actually work in either SAP or Oracle to see how dis-integrated their applications actually are. The illusion is so effective that it even fools software vendors that compete with SAP or Oracle. I can recall my great surprise when I analyzed the prebuilt adapter that extracted information from SAP ERP b SAP BI/BW. It was clear that Development had done the absolute minimum required in order to mislead potential customers into thinking that they could pull a large variety of data from SAP ERP into BI/BW. Instead, what customers really received was a starter kit. Customers received the worst of both worlds, market place lagging functionality at a premium price, a premium cost for consulting along with a greatly underestimated implementation expense as the vast majority of the integration between SAP ERP and BI/BW had to be built.

Companies like SAP and Oracle promptly took full advantage of this market power, and this enabled them to charge top dollar for all of their applications, and furthermore, to easily compete with applications that were **far superior** to their own applications. Overall, this power was abused in so many ways that it would be tedious for my readers if I listed them all. But I will mention one of the more creative ways, which was developed by SAP: their pseudo partnership program with other vendors promised entry into SAP's enormous client database,[16] when in fact, the program was a giant **intelligence-gathering** operation by SAP to allow it to steal intellectual property from their "partner" vendors, thus helping them to backward engineer the application (this was called the xApps program,

---

[15] In the case of Microsoft, their applications actually did work better than competing applications on Windows, although they often made sure of this by postponing information about Windows from becoming public until the new version of Windows was released—they could have very easily released the APIs earlier.

[16] Which happened very rarely.

which I describe in the article below). As far as I can see, SCM Focus was the only media entity to call this program what it was.

http://www.scmfocus.com/inventoryoptimizationmultiechelon/2010/01/its-time-for-the-sap-xapps-program-to-die/

http://www.scmfocus.com/enterprisesoftwarepolicy/2012/01/27/how-common-is-it-for-sap-to-take-intellectual-property-from-partners/[17]

Once again the IT/business press and IT analysts failed to explain what this program actually was, and, in fact, they lauded it. And once again they were proven incorrect when the program died and did not lead to a new golden age of integrated applications (no surprise, it was never intended to, it was never more than an intellectual property vaccum cleaner).

The upshot of all of this was that the ERP vendors were in an excellent position to sell more software into these accounts. These new non-ERP applications all have their own platforms, and while they have adapters or interfaces to one another, they are each a separate application; they each have a different database and sit on different hardware. In fact, many of these new applications are acquisitions: after a software vendor acquires another software vendor, they typically develop a marketing program to inform all current and potential customers as to how well the new applications will work together. ERP clients who purchased applications that Oracle had acquired were actually worse off than if the software had been **left independent and adapters had been written to Oracle ERP.** The long-term history of software acquisition clearly demonstrates that as the price of software goes up, development of the application stalls, and in many cases the application is simply subsumed into what is often an inferior application. There are a number of cases where the acquired application is mostly eliminated. But the acquiring company also acquires the customers and is able to increase their

---

[17] As is the norm, the Federal Trade Commission (the government entity responsible for enforcing anti-trust legislation) does nothing in the enterprise software space but rubber-stamp its approval of acquisitions. There is little incentive for the FTC to enforce anti-trust laws that most of the US population does not know exist, and when members of the FTC are actually looking for jobs in the companies that they supposedly regulate. Like the SEC, the FTC is an excellent place to network and to obtain well-paying jobs in the industry.

prices now that they have removed a competitor from the marketplace. Software acquisitions have only two winners:

1. *The Acquiring Company:* They eliminate a competitor.

2. *The Senior Members of the Acquired Firm:* They receive a handsome buy-out as compensation.

Despite promises on the part of the acquiring vendor, often the reality for integration does not change very much after an acquisition. For example, many of these software vendors already had adapters that connected to Oracle ERP. However, the acquisitions allowed Oracle to increase the price of the acquired application because they became part of the "Oracle Suite." If a major vendor could not either kill a competitor or charge more for the acquired application—why would the acquiring vendor make the acquisition? The answer is they couldn't because it would not pay.

As a result, companies that implemented ERP are essentially back where they started before the move to ERP, except now they rely more on external application development through commercial software rather than internal application development. While buying companies were sold on the idea that ERP would take a "blank sheet of paper" approach, to the present day companies *still* have complex landscapes with many applications that have separate databases and separate hardware and are **interfaced**, but not **integrated—just like before the whole ERP trend began**. Promises of a single integrated system simply never came about.

One Size Fits All

One of the original arguments used to sell ERP systems was that the standard functionality of the ERP system could be used *"right out of the box."* But as ERP systems are customized so regularly, this sales pitch has long since been forgotten. Not only was this assumption wrong, it was fabulously wrong. According to research by Mint Jurtras, around **96 percent of respondents to a survey** stated that they did moderate to extensive customization to their ERP systems. This has been my experience on projects as well, but I can say with confidence that most companies that purchased ERP systems had no idea they would eventually customize their ERP systems to the degree that they did.

At one of my defense contractor clients I discussed their interest in replacing a system that connected to the Department of Defense. At first it seemed as if we could take the logic for the system and port it to SAP ERP. However, the more we analyzed the application, the more it became apparent that this application was so specialized and had taken so much time and effort to build that the best course of action was simply to keep the system but integrate it to SAP ERP.

Over the decades, many companies have gone through this identical process. It looks much easier to decommission software when you do not personally use it and are not aware of everything that it does.[18] Very little is written on the subject of system replacement errors, which led IT decision-makers to greatly underestimate the degree to which companies faced this issue of being unable to decommission systems that were performing important tasks, and to **overestimate how well the ERP implementations at other companies were faring**. Companies bought ERP, often without knowing how specialized their own applications were, and they ended up having to integrate many more systems to the ERP system than they had expected, as well as to customize their ERP systems more than they ever anticipated. As a result, their ERP systems consumed a much higher percentage of their IT budgets than forecasted.

All of the above happened, but to a much larger degree, on the Air Force's Expeditionary Combat Support System (ECSS) initiative, a now notorious program to take all of the Air Force's support systems (240 legacy systems) and move them to Oracle ERP. Some salespeople at Oracle, with the help of Computer Sciences Corporation (CSC), essentially convinced the Air Force that they could replace almost all of the supply chain and accounting systems maintained by the Air Force with their ERP system. One billion dollars later, the Air Force finally concluded that their project objective was not possible; further extraordinary customization would have been required, which would have taken another **one billion to**

---

[18] The proposal that all these customized applications could be replaced by generic ERP systems was ludicrous, but was accepted by decision makers precisely because they lacked familiarity with their own systems.

complete. Therefore the Air Force cancelled ECSS. The functionality to replicate the Air Force's existing systems did not exist in Oracle ERP; CSC and Oracle would have been required to both generalize the Air Force's processes and rebuild a truly huge quantity of custom functionality in Oracle.

If there ever was a project doomed before it even began, it was the ECSS project. The Air Force bought the *"we can cover all your requirements"* argument pitched by ERP salespeople and consulting companies in the most extreme way. Think about this: Oracle ERP can cover 240 systems encompassing decades of specialized development? That is quite a proposal. But to various degrees, most other companies have fallen for the same argument. This inability to use "out of the box" ERP functionality is a theme that is often repeated, as explained in the quotation below:

> *"… many mid-sized companies quickly find that different business units have slightly different requirements, even for commodity processes like accounts payable and human resources. These local differences may arise from regulatory and compliance considerations, or simply a resistance to changing current working practices because of the organizational impact. Faced with inherent limitations and no viable way to overcome them, the team responsible for expanding a legacy ERP implementation is often forced to create multiple ERP instances (each with its own database), resulting in:*
> - *Dramatically increased cost, complexity and effort for corporate reporting and analytics*
> - *Added complexity to support transactions among business units*
> - *Increased hardware and IT administration cost and complexity*
> - *A natural tendency toward local optimization at the expense of overall visibility and effectiveness"* — Is Your ERP Creating a Legacy of Frustration?

Planning for the Inevitable Customization

Unanticipated customization greatly increases implementation costs and durations. It also means long-term and largely unanticipated maintenance as the customized

ERP systems face issues caused by each new version (or at least major version) of the ERP software released by the vendor. The customization required for ERP systems has demonstrated that these systems are **simply starter kits** rather than completely usable systems. Companies went to tremendous expense to do nothing more than replicate functionality that was, in many cases, working perfectly well and meeting requirements in the legacy applications that ERP salespeople criticized as archaic. The reality is that the ERP salespeople had no idea what they were talking about, and, in fact, never cared. Most had never worked in the field of software implementation and, like trained parrots, were simply repeating catch phrases. And the scary thought is that it fooled so may executives within implementing companies. The term arrogance is greatly overused—often being applied to a person with strong domain expertise as a leveling mechanism. However, if there is a better use of the term than in this situation I am unaware of what it could be. It is arrogance to state that you "know" that the functionality in your software is better than the functionality residing in a customer's system, when you have never seen nor analyzed their system and probably would not understand it if you did.

The Single Instance Logic of ERP

Another main selling point of ERP was that a company would be able to move to a single instance of their ERP system. This idea continues to be a selling point of vendors such as SAP, even though **in most cases only smaller companies actually have single instances of ERP.**

> "An 'instance' refers to the number of discreet versions of ERP software you have in your company. The original vision of ERP was that companies should have a single instance—that is, a single implementation of the software running on a single database—that serves the entire company. It would mean no duplication of information in different departments or in different geographic divisions and thus better integration and information quality across the company. Upgrading the software would also be easier than with multiple customized instances of ERP across the company." — The ABCs of ERP

Historically, companies have been unable to move to a single instance of ERP, yet so few people have asked why this is the case, especially since this is presented as such a desirable end state. As the complexity of a company increases with the addition of regions or subsidiaries, the value of having a single instance of an ERP system becomes questionable. Vendors certainly know this, but present a single instance as a desirable option with benefits to the customer in any case.

The reasons why companies are unable to move to a single ERP instance are well documented and are not going away; some of the major causes are listed below:

1. *Database Management and Query Efficiency:* ERP systems are supposed to be single database systems, which belies their integration. There are issues with reduced efficiencies at higher data volumes, but what is the value of having sales figures from different subsidiaries that may have no relationship to each other in the same sales order table? For instance, if a user performs a query for all sales in a quarter, do they mean the sales of subsidiary one or subsidiary two? How do proponents of the single instance ERP system consider the increased complexity of the data in their presentation of this solution?

2. *Which Region/Division/Subsidiary Gets Its Way?:* If different regions do business differently, and they must move to a single instance, which region gets the system configured or customized to its requirements? What happens to the productivity of the company that gets its configuration adjusted for no other reason than the desire to normalize the functionality across the subsidiaries so that the move to a single ERP system can be facilitated? Most often it is the region with the political power (i.e., the region where the headquarters are located), and has absolutely nothing to do with logic or what is best for the business. I have been on several global implementations and I would recommend to any independent contractor who could choose between a global implementation and a regional implementation to choose the latter. Global implementations are exercises in one region enforcing its will upon the other regions. At one client site, the region with the headquarters simply left out functionality that was available in the application when the new application was explained to the other regions. The functionality they left out would have allowed the application to be configured differently. They did this to prevent the other region from choosing a configuration that was different from what they had already decided upon. The region that selected the configuration

assumed that the configuration was right for everyone seeing as **they** had selected it. They called this the "Global Template," which was a convenient way of getting the other regions to do things their way.

3. *Negotiation Leverage:* A single ERP system is viewed as a cost savings because more business is aggregated to one vendor. Surely this is a one-sided view on the matter: single sourcing also increases the negotiating leverage of the vendor (why they like it so much). What happens when the ERP vendor knows they have 100 percent of a customer's ERP business? Well, this is just the starting point for Tier 1 ERP vendors; their eventual goal is to replace all enterprise software used by the company with their other applications, to turn the client's IT infrastructure into a monoculture, and to staff the IT departments with 100 percent compliant executive decision-makers. If this sounds vaguely familiar, it is because it is the same desire of every major IT consulting company. When I first got into consulting my partner at KPMG explained to me that our role was to "penetrate" the client and then "radiate" through them.

4. *What About Functionality?:* Looking from 30,000 feet up, it's easy to state, *"If we use one system we can save money."* However, there is another side of the equation: the value that the system provides. When a company moves to a monoculture, having regions/divisions/subsidiaries—the people who actually know the business, reduces the functionality benefits—choose their own solutions. This leads to the next point.

5. *How Much Does Customization Increase With a Single Solution?:* Proponents of a single instance ERP leave this point out of the analysis, and for good reason. Using a single instance ERP system will mean more customization or, as so many IT proponents prefer, taking a wrecking ball to the business requirements. However, customization translates to real money, both up front and in long-term maintenance, and the costs must be estimated as part of a strategy of moving to a single instance ERP.

6. *What About Flexibility?:* Moving toward a single ERP system has negative implications for the flexibility of the company. If the acquisition is eventually sold, what is the cost of breaking the acquisition out from the combined ERP system?

This may not be a big surprise, Tier 1 ERP vendors are not doing this analysis—or have done the analysis but don't want their customers to know the truth. Instead they continue to **bang the gong** of single instance ERP. In truth, that a single ERP system was never a realistic proposition should have been apparent to buyers from the very beginning. It is now well documented that the vast majority of companies **do not** have a single ERP system, and the reasons are quite well explained. The following quote is just one of many examples.

> *"Well, it sounded great on paper, but unfortunately reality bites. The stories started to leak out—multi-million dollar never-ending ERP projects, high profile ERP project failures, inability to tailor the deployment to local subsidiary needs, and over-tapped local IT resources overwhelmed by a monolithic on-premises ERP deployment. And if a division is run as a profit-center, these kinds of deployments can quickly paint red all over the P&L."* — The Decline of Single Instance ERP

Multiple ERP systems in companies are now the norm, and not just two or three ERP systems as the quotation below explains.

> *"On average, big companies worldwide are running five SAP instances, while almost four in ten have more than six, according to a study from IT services firm HCL Technologies."* — When SAP Sprawl is Cool, ZDNet

> *"The concept of a single monolithic system failed for many companies. Different divisions or facilities often made independent purchases, and other systems were inherited through mergers and acquisitions. Thus, many companies ended up having several instances of the same ERP systems or a variety of different ERP systems altogether, further complicating their IT landscape. In the end, ERP systems became just another subset of the legacy systems they were supposed to replace."* — The Trouble with Enterprise Software

According to one IDC survey, 72 percent of respondents were running more than one ERP system. People will say that multiple ERP instances can be consolidated into one, but in most cases that is simply not practical. There are a number of very good reasons as to why a company cannot reasonably be expected to move to a single ERP instance.

> *"'A lot of people run multiple instances because of geographic reasons, regulations, or business-sector reasons,' Illsley said.*

> *"If you've got part of your business that is outsourced, for example, you'd probably want to run an instance that your outsourcing provider could use and that would be different to the one you would want to keep inside, so that it's easier to do things like that." —* When SAP Sprawl is Cool, ZDNet

So, while some companies have moved to a single instance of ERP, most have not and will not in the future. It is easier for smaller companies to move to a single instance, and more difficult for larger companies, particularly companies with subsidiaries. We are now three decades into the ERP phenomena and only a small portion of single instance ERP systems are in use. So why is it still considered a realistic goal to move to a single instance of ERP? Apparently many Tier 1 ERP software vendors think it is quite reasonable. However many companies are turning a deaf ear to this message and are, in fact, now far more frequently exploring the concept of a two-tiered ERP system.

The Logic of Cost Reduction for ERP

All of the above factors undermine a primary argument used to sell ERP systems which is that ERP systems **reduce** overall IT costs. After the ERP market had become saturated, the cost reduction logic "declined as a point of emphasis," because the vendors were now motivated to sell different types of software. The storyline of Tier 1 ERP vendors changes continually depending upon what they have to sell at the time.

ERP systems were supposed to save companies money through the standardization of business processes. ERP customers generally accepted this without question. The quotation below provides an example of the pitch.

> *"It is also one of the most worthwhile initiatives for securing your place in a competitive market. A successful, enterprise-wide implementation will move your company from one with piece-meal business procedures and no overall plan, to a re-engineered organization that is poised to take growth and profitability to a whole new level."* — Why ERP is Vital to Productivity and Profitability

This is an example of a generic argument that proposes that businesses were somehow lost in the wilderness, lacking direction until—**POOF!** ERP came to save them from themselves.[19] The next quotation is a more sophisticated explanation for what is still a flawed appraisal of the situation.

> *"Many organizations have several different legacy systems that have developed over the years to meet their information needs for planning and decision making. Often there is little or no integration among departments and applications used by separate departments do not communicate with each other. This means that data has to be entered into each separate department of the organization resulting in data redundancy and at times inaccuracy. ERP systems can virtually eliminate the redundancies that occur from these outdated and separate systems. ERP systems integrate various systems into one and data is entered into the system only once."* — What Managers Should Know About ERP and ERP II

It's hard to fathom why these companies had not already created interfaces between their applications. As has been explained in both "The Integration Logic for ERP" and "The Single Instance Logic for ERP" sections of this chapter, not only are

---

[19] Coincidentally, this also follows the narrative of a Harvard Business School Case Study, where a business is in shambles but is saved by a Harvard MBA who rectifies all of the problems with some outstanding management changes. Problem solved. In the standard case study, sometimes the MBA wears a cape, and sometimes not.

there many other applications that must be interfaced to ERP, but often multiple ERP systems must be interfaced to one another. Therefore ERP has not *"virtually eliminated the redundancies that occur from separate systems."* We have the same redundancies and the same issues, except we **have newer systems**. The above quote seems to have been written by someone who does not spend any time on actual projects, because those who have work experience in this area have come to the opposite conclusion.

As far as systems being outdated, one of the major complaints of ERP clients is that their ERP vendors have stabilized the functionality within their ERP systems and are no longer innovating. This was **the same complaint regarding legacy systems and the reasons they were called outdated!**

Here is another quotation that contains more unexamined assumptions.

> *"ERP systems are based on a value chain view of the business where functional departments coordinate their work, focus on value-adding activities and eliminate redundancy. ERP can be a valuable tool for managers to improve operational as well as financial performance of the firm."* — What Managers Should Know About ERP and ERP II

This sounds great; however, how would the author know this? A lot of things "could be" but I have searched through all of the research on this topic and there is no evidence of this. In fact, the ROI is so low, that companies have had to **change their stories as to why they implemented ERP**, often turning to the equally fallacious argument that ERP improved integration in their companies (as highlighted in the following quote).[20]

> *"ERP systems replace complex and sometimes manual interfaces between different systems with standardized, cross-functional transaction automation."* — The Impact of Enterprise Systems on Corporate Performance

---

[20] As I was writing this book, I often joked with friends that following up on the many false statements made about ERP is like chasing a squirrel around a tree. As soon as one argument is disproved, another argument is presented in a chained sequence until you end up back at the original argument.

I have to ask how current this observation is and whether it still applies, or whether it was ever true. This paper was written in 2005, but interfaces between systems do the same thing that ERP does, and have for many years.

Conclusion

This chapter goes back to the origin of the ERP in order to analyze how ERP was justified in the first place. This is important, because it turns out that the proposals contained within the two tier ERP concept contradict the logic used to sell ERP systems. The proponents of two tier ERP have hoped, and have been rewarded in that hope, that the recipients of the message did not notice the inconsistency. ERP systems have no reduced costs, as was predicted by both consulting companies and by ERP vendors. ERP systems have not reduced the number of instances of different software that are used by companies.

All of these logics are similar in that they were over simplifications of reality, and none of them were ever actually proven true. They were never hypotheses that were formulated to be tested. They were proposals that were designed to help pave the way for software and consulting purchases. The evidence is clear that none of the logics were proven to be correct, and yet there is almost a total blackout of this fact. Academic research shows this, but exceedingly few have addressed the discrepancy between the official storyline on ERP and the research. Instead the logics presented in this chapter continue to be used in order to sell more software and consulting. This displays a concerning inability of corporate buyers to differentiate between evidence based statements and marketing propaganda. In the next chapter we will explain the total cost of ownership of ERP systems—which is directly related to the logic of whether ERP systems reduce costs.

CHAPTER 5

Analyzing Two-tiered ERP

The first thing to consider when understanding what to do with two-tiered ERP is that two-tiered ERP is **not** new. Two-tiered or multiple-tiered ERP has been used since ERP systems were initially sold. What is new is the marketing of the concept: the use of multiple ERP systems from different vendors is a way of improving the value returned from ERP implementations.

The Unstated Assumption of Two-tiered ERP

What is unsaid regarding two-tiered ERP may be even more interesting. The story that is being told regarding two-tiered ERP is not the full story; instead, it is an engineering/marketing construct that only tells part of the story. Tier 2 and Tier 3 ERP vendors don't dare contradict the established viewpoint that Tier 1 ERP software is necessary, even though it isn't. Software vendors don't want a lot of controversy or "trouble"—they just want to sell software.

Thus the Tier 2 and Tier 3 vendors have developed the two-tiered concept as an adjunct to a centralized ERP system. The vendors have presented this digestible new strategy without undermining the sacred cow of Tier 1 ERP, which would be off-putting to companies that have spent so much money on tier 1 ERP systems and have so little to show for it. The two-tiered ERP concept allows Tier 2 and Tier 3 ERP vendors to tiptoe around what makes the two-tiered strategy work—unlike other ERP "savior concepts" that have come before it such as rapid big ERP implementation methodologies (an oxymoron if there ever was one) or service oriented architecture (i.e. SOA—a philosophy that Tier 1 vendors had zero interest in supporting).

Hopefully this book has provided enough information to convince you that two-tiered ERP both a) makes sense and b) is nothing new. However, if one accepts the premise that two-tiered ERP is worthwhile, the question becomes what to do about it. A big part of this decision is determining **who** to listen to; so many entities in the market claim theirs is the right course to follow with respect to two-tiered ERP. However, very few of these vendors could be considered financially unbiased, and none provide any evidence to support these claims.

Let's start off by listening to what the Tier 1 vendors have to say on the topic.

The Tier 1 ERP Software Vendors

Tier 1 ERP software vendors have attempted to co-opt and change how two-tiered ERP is implemented. Let's remember that the original idea behind two-tiered ERP was to implement **below Tier 1 ERP applications** into subsidiaries and sub-companies that had lower functionality demands than the parent company. Two-tiered ERP was initially presented as a way to reduce cost and complexity, to which the Tier 1 ERP companies say:

> *"Great, we are on board. Just implement multiple instances of our Tier 1 software."*

However, that is **not** a two-tiered ERP strategy: that is a multi-instance ERP strategy using the same software. Tier 1 ERP vendors counter this argument with their second proposal:

> *"We offer mid-market ERP systems also, so use our mid-market solutions for the other tiers."*

At Software Decisions, full TCO analysis was performed on both SAP and Oracle Tier 2 "mid-market" solutions. Depending upon whether the vendor is SAP or Oracle, **the cost savings can be lower or about the same as other well-known Tier 2 ERP applications**. However, adjusting for more than costs, the argument is actually better for SAP, as they have a far more capable Tier 2 ERP application in SAP Business One than does Oracle in Oracle JD Edwards World. Both software vendors propose that they offer a better value versus alteratives that do not offer both a tier 1 and teir 2 ERP application, as their respective tier 1 and tier 2 ERP systems are integrated to one another or share a common heritage. However, a close examination of each software vendor's system calls this assertion into question. SAP's Tier 1 offering (called ECC or R/3) has nothing at all to do with SAP Business One, their Tier 2 offering. SAP Business One was not developed by SAP but was renamed after SAP acquired TopManage Financial Systems, along with TopManage's sister company TopTier. As such SAP Business One has a completely different technical heritage than SAP ECC. And while SAP will no doubt advise that it has some adapters that connect SAP ECC to SAP Business One, the connection benefits between these systems should be viewed with great skepticism if previous experience with SAP's integration claims are any indication.

Both of Oracle's main ERP systems—Oracle JD Edwards EnterpriseOne and Oracle JD Edwards World—were the result of acquisitions and were not developed by Oracle. Regardless of any integration that exists between the systems, Oracle JD Edwards World is an application that should be retired as it is not a viable option for future purchases.

SAP and Oracle—knowing they have limited ability to stop a customer set on the concept from moving to a two-tiered ERP strategy—would like to steer customers in a direction that benefits SAP and Oracle. Rather than performing a proper software selection, SAP and Oracle would like their customers to simply choose the solutions that SAP and Oracle want them to choose. Once again they will argue that their systems will integrate better with their tier 1 ERP systems, an arguement that we discredited in the previous section. Even if integration were not an issue, their solution may not be a good decision as it's unlikely the proposed application is the best fit for the company's business requirement. Secondly, integrating the lower-tier ERP systems into a master ERP system is only one way of implementing two-tiered ERP. Another, less costly, approach is simply to integrate all the ERP systems to a master business intelligence system. Many ERP vendors leave this alterantive out when discussing two tier ERP with potential clients. However, integrateing to the master business intelligence system is, in my view, a preferable solution architecture.

Biased "Advice" from Tier 1 ERP Vendors

It's unclear why **anyone** would listen to Tier 1 ERP software vendors on the topic of two-tiered ERP. Their only interest is to redirect purchases back to their applications, and so any of their opinions or recommendations are based simply on their marketing and sales function. They are countering a movement in the marketplace with the tools they have available. Furthermore, nothing that either SAP or Oracle has predicted on the topic of ERP has ever turned out to be true.

Bill Maher lampooned those who promoted the Iraq War.

> *"If you're someone from one of the think tanks that dreamed up the Iraq War, who predicted that we would be greeted as liberators, and that we would not need a lot of troops, and that the Iraqi oil would pay for the war, that the WMDs would be found, that the looting was not problematic, that the mission was accomplished, that the insurgency was in its last throws, that things would get better after the people voted, after the government was formed, after we got Saddam, after we got his kids, after we got Zarqawi, and that the whole bloody mess would not turn into a civil war...you have to stop making predictions."*

The same could be said for Tier 1 ERP software vendors. Buyers that have followed the advice of SAP or Oracle in setting up their solution architecture have resulted in the highest cost, and lowest functionality corporate IT infrastructures, as is explained in the Software Decisions Solution Architecture TCO studies.

http://www.scmfocus.com/softwaredecisions/plans/solution-architecture-packages/

SAP routinely spins false marketing constructs that have little to do with reality, such as NetWeaver and HANA. Oracle's internal culture of lying runs so deep that other software vendors point to it as a **reason to increase their own lying**. Many marketing departments have put effort into developing literature regarding their position on two-tiered ERP, with the single intent of getting you to think they have the best approach to two-tiered ERP. Much of the information provided by Tier 2 and Tier 3 ERP software vendors is of a dubious nature, as demonstrated by the following quotation from Sage, a Tier 2 ERP software vendor:

> *"Well-run, global organizations are increasingly adopting a two-tier enterprise resource planning (ERP) strategy."*

If one were to read through the source paper of this quote, one would note that this bold pronouncement is never supported by any evidence. The statement is not, *"Increasingly a few well-run, global organizations are adopting...";* the statement is categorical. In fact, the only evidence presented throughout the paper is that two-tier ERP is becoming a topic of greater interest among corporate buyers. This is a problem, because the paper implies that it has evidence that two-tiered ERP is what good companies implement as will be demonstrated at some point in the paper (but never is).

As I have said in this book, two-tiered ERP **does** make sense due to the high cost and poor performance of Tier 1 ERP. However, there is a difference between something appearing logical and stating that better companies are employing the strategy.

> *"Organizations in the market for ERP solutions are increasingly considering a two-tier ERP strategy. A recent study by Constellation Research found that forty-eight percent of buyers in 2011 were considering a two-tier strategy, up sharply from thirty-two percent in 2010 and twenty-seven percent in 2009"* [21]

The above statement is a standard way to begin a promotional paper of this type. However, the statement does not demonstrate whether a two-tier strategy

---

[21] From Sage white paper, *Why Implement a Two-tiered ERP Strategy.*

has actually worked in practice. Instead it merely provides evidence that more companies are focused on the question. This increased interest could be due to any number of reasons, such as the enormous quantity of marketing literature produced by software vendors and the prevelance of conference sessions on the topic. The article goes on to trace the supposed roots of two-tiered ERP.

> *"Two-tier ERP systems began their rise in popularity during the economic recession that began in late 2008. As IT budgets were slashed, IT departments were forced to make do with less. In many cases, large-scale ERP migration plans were delayed or eliminated entirely. Instead of moving to new systems, companies focused on improving existing systems, including legacy ERP applications. As a result, many organizations decided to retain functionality in their existing systems that were still working while migrating to Tier 2 systems where existing solutions were not meeting their requirements."*

This paragraph is not true. The popularity of two-tiered EPR did not rise during the economic recession of 2008. Two-tiered ERP has always been used for one reason: generally Tier 1 ERP is too expensive for subdivisions, and companies never moved to single instance Tier 1 ERP.[22] This entire paragraph is confusing and apparently the author does not know the history of ERP. Instead of being based in the history of ERP, this paragraph attempts to develop a narrative where Tier 2 ERP is a significant trend, and to give the impression that two-tier ERP is entirely new. The paper goes on to say:.

> *"At the same time, organizations began realizing that big-bang, corporatewide ERP installations are often ineffective. When a system becomes very large, it becomes costly to customize, maintain, and upgrade."*

For some time SCM Focus has proposed that an incremental implementation strategy be used even within one application—rolling out less complex functionality

---

[22] *This is explained by Gartner in the following quotation. "As a result, it is far more frequently true that a subset of the ERP suite—usually administrative functions, such as finance, HR and indirect procurement—becomes the focus of the single-vendor, single-instance strategy."*

earlier. Generally this approach is not followed. Implementation methods tend to change little over the years, in that they rarely reflect what has worked or not worked historically. Since I began working on IT implementations in 1997, I have seen little adjustment to implementation methodologies. No evidence is presented in the paper that companies are moving away from big bang implementations. I could find no research that even studied the movement of companies away from big bang IT implementations to incremental IT implementations.

The Sage paper goes on to say that two-tiered ERP is being driven by changes in corporate structures.

> *"For example, many organizations have undergone multiple mergers and acquisitions that leave them with multiple ERP solutions—and unacceptable support costs."*

There is nothing at all new about this, except for the fact that support costs from the Tier 1 ERP vendors have been increasing steadily. However, multiple companies being part of another company, all with different ERP systems, is why two-tiered or multi-tiered ERP has become a popular "strategy" since ERP systems first began being used in the mid 1980s—although calling it a "strategy" may be giving it too much credit for forethought. Rather, the strategy resulted from circumstances.

The Sage paper goes on to report that many respondents to a survey believe that Tier 1 ERP systems are expensive.

> *"Seventy percent of respondents to a recent Software Insider survey remarked that existing, Tier 1 systems are too expensive. An estimate published by CIO magazine in 2009 placed the cost of the average Tier 1 ERP system deployment at between $13 million and $17 million. ROI calculation on Tier 1 ERP systems show that high costs are due to overruns in implementation, customization, maintenance fees, and staff costs. Upgrade costs are also high—45 percent of respondents said that upgrades are too costly."*

Yes, the survey results reflect reality, but are presented in the article as if they represent new information. In fact, the only new part to this is that support fees have increased. Tier 1 ERP systems have been known to be quite expensive for decades.

> *"When all of the implementation, ongoing maintenance fees, upgrades, and modifications are considered, a two-tiered system can offer significant financial savings. For example, Gartner Research found that companies see a thirty-three percent reduction in implementation costs when a two-tier system is deployed."*

Firstly, our research at Software Decisions is quite a bit more thorough than Gartner's because we estimate the cost savings for the entire TCO of a two-tiered ERP strategy—and we have tested a number of scenarios. Our research shows that a thirty-three percent reduction in TCO costs is the upper end of the cost savings continuum, while a predicted TCO cost savings in the twelve perent to seventeen percent range is a more reasonable expectation. However, it depends upon the size of the Tier 1 ERP system as compared to the Tier 2 ERP system.

Obviously, Tier 1 ERP systems are bad values. Any other strategy, such as using a best-of-breed application (even a best-of-breed finance application), will yield far better financial outcomes. All this seems to beg the following question: If Tier 1 ERP systems are so expensive, why have they been recommended by Gartner and the major consulting companies for more than three decades? (Hint: It's not because Tier 1 ERP provides good value to customers. No research has ever produced a positive return on investment for Tier 1 ERP.) So, whose interests are these entities looking out for, if not the customer's?

Sage presents a lot of information, but seems interested in drawing only one conclusion: the answer is two-tiered ERP. In doing so, they leave out other conclusions that are just as interesting and important to analyze. The Sage paper goes on to highlight a well-known issue regarding Tier 1 ERP systems and innovation.

> *"Yet thirty-five percent of Software Insider survey participants found that enterprise-class ERP vendors have not innovated quickly enough.*

Subsidiaries are finding that they can customize Tier 2 applications more quickly than they can convince corporate to change the global ERP system to meet their local needs."

This is also true. Tier 1 ERP software vendors have been using their ERP applications as cash cows for more than a decade and a half. They use the high profits from their ERP systems to acquire or develop non-ERP applications, which they then sell into their customer bases, acquiring a higher and higher percentage of their customers' IT budgets. Again, who are the culprits for this end result? Those who recommended Tier 1 ERP systems as necessary: the major consulting companies and Gartner (who is used repeatedly as a source in the Sage article), as well as other analysts who told companies that Tier 1 ERP **would lead to great things**.

The Sage article goes on to praise the speed with which Tier 2 ERP applications can be implemented.

"A two-tiered infrastructure can be deployed quickly and cost effectively. The time to implement and modify or upgrade is likely to be shorter, which means that deploying such a system will deliver a shorter time-to-benefit, and these systems can be modified more quickly and easily than a Tier 1 ERP solution."

This could be filed under the category of "self-evident." This quotation again states that Tier 1 ERP software is inefficient and expensive to operate. Of course, anything—with the possible exception of lagging business intelligence applications (i.e., IBM Cognos, SAP BI, Oracle BI)—are going to seem efficient compared to Tier 1 ERP, which brings up again the question of why Tier 1 ERP is used in the first place.

Marketing Does not Equal Reality

Just because a vendor has invested in marketing literature about two-tiered ERP, does **not mean they are a good choice** for your two-tiered or multi-tiered ERP strategy. In fact, an ERP vendor's position or marketing material on two-tiered ERP is immaterial to any purchasing decision. Different ERP systems are fundamentally separate. At Software Decisions, we have evaluated thirteen ERP systems, and none of these ERP systems were designed to be integrated to other ERP systems. Gartner states this, albeit more delicately.

> *"Do not assume that integration between systems will be plug-and-play, even if provided by the same vendor."*

The vendors of some of the better ERP systems that we have reviewed have not written any marketing literature on two-tiered ERP. Conversely, some of the lowest-scoring ERP on systems include the most literature on two-tiered ERP. Any company that intends to use a variety of ERP software vendors can simply use the same software selection approach that tends to result in the best software being selected. No review of the various literature on two-tiered ERP is necessary.[23]

Major Consulting Companies

The major consulting companies don't have much interest in promoting two-tiered ERP because their main interest is in billing for tier 1 ERP resources; resources for lower tier ERP bill out at a lower rate. Furthermore, there are more software vendor options, and major consulting companies are not interested in retraining or hiring new resources so that they can bill hours. So the "recommendation" of major consulting companies on two-tiered ERP will be that it is *"too early to jump in,"* and that two-tiered ERP will take resources away from the really important work of *"improving the tier 1 ERP system and moving toward a single instance."* Not surprisingly Accenture published a document entitled *"Why Big Systems Are Here to Stay,"* which perhaps should have been called *"Why Big Systems Are Here to Stay: Because We Make Tons of Money That Way."* In this document, Accenture makes the following contentions:

> *"And a third advantage of an ERP environment has to do with how data is managed, integrated and secured. If not properly integrated, cloud and software-as-a-service solutions can create a more chaotic, less reliable and less secure data environment."*

---

[23] Exactly how to do this is covered in the SCM Focus Press book, *Enterprise Software Selection: How to Pinpoint the Perfect Software Solution using Multiple Information Sources.*

This is an interesting assertion, because ERP environments have zero advantage over non-ERP environments with respect to data management, integration or security. ERP systems that I evaluated often had the lowest data quality of any software category—particularly for the Tier 1 ERP vendors as the applications have such dated data management tools. As for integration, ERP systems may be integrated to themselves, but the Tier 1 ERP vendors are some of the most difficult systems to integrate with other applications. As for the security argument, ERP systems are not more secure than other software categories.

The above Accenture statement also confuses the topic of ERP systems versus SaaS systems. SaaS is a delivery method for software; ERP is a category of enterprise software. SaaS can deliver as an on-premises solution for any application, including ERP. ERP systems that are on-premises are more secure than cloud or SaaS applications, but that is a different issue.

Overall, the evidence to support the statement made in the Accenture paper is severely lacking, and it should qualify as FUD (fear, uncertainty and doubt). Accenture has a financial incentive to slow the movement away from Tier 1 ERP and toward SaaS solutions because it's how they make a lot of money: they have far less control once the application is delivered via SaaS. With SaaS, the software vendor tends to take over consulting and support. Interestingly, nowhere in the paper does Accenture mention how it makes money (which is with on-premises consulting and support) and how this may influence its "recommendations."

Accenture goes on to say that the best approach is a hybrid: some on-premises and some SaaS. They then proceed to make another self-serving proposal, that this IT ecology must be managed by using a trusted "broker."

> *"So, who's in charge of managing this complex hybrid system? The answer lies in the rising trend of using an integrator or trusted broker. This brokerage can act as either a consultant or as a managed services provider. This holistic or managed services approach enables companies to treat their IT resources as just that and also provides a new level of flexibility for companies and CIOs."*

And who would be this trusted broker? That's right—Accenture! After spending decades overcharging and misdirecting their clients to all the wrong software in the on-premises environment, Accenture would like to be handed the keys to managing their clients' IT solution architecture in the new on-premises/SaaS "hybrid" environment.

The major consulting companies don't really have "opinions" on topics; all they see is whatever maximizes their revenues. It's very simple: two-tiered ERP along with SaaS-delivered software reduces their revenues—therefore, they are against it. Now, if what I am saying is true, why would Accenture develop a partnership with NetSuite, as the links below describe?

http://www.netsuite.com/portal/landing/accenture.shtml

http://www.oracle.com/us/corporate/press/1966087

Generally, partnership statements of this kind are not reliable indicators regarding a policy within the consulting companies. Companies develop partnerships all the time, and many of them do not extend beyond the marketing press release and the insertion of company logos on one another's websites.

Both software vendors and consulting companies love having partnership logos on one another's websites. However, in most cases these partnerships are much less than meets the eye. I cover this topic in the following article about the overused and often meaningless integration certifications that many smaller software vendors have on their websites that show some integration to a major ERP software vendor.

http://www.scmfocus.com/sapintegration/2011/11/15/what-are-saps-vendor-integration-certifications-worth-on-projects/

A far better indicator of how dedicated a company is to a particular strategy or line of business is whether they put out marketing collateral on the topic. And the major consulting companies have not done this—at least at the time this book was published. If their clients demand that they provide Tier 2 and Tier 3 resources, the major consulting companies will do it; after all, they prefer to have the business rather than to lose the business, but they would prefer not to do this.

IT Analysts

Having read the reports of several analysts on two-tiered ERP, it was interesting to see their take on the topic. IT analysts have not spent space in print explaining the history of ERP to their subscribers. Some of them use phrases such as, *"two-tiered ERP can be effective if implemented properly,"* which sounds authoritative. As there are no studies on the effectiveness of two-tiered ERP, this statement sounds quite fabricated unless they can provide the evidence to back it up. Statements like this provide a nice escape hatch for IT analysts. If the trend does well, the analyst can say, *"I predicted it,"* and if two-tiered ERP does not work well, the analyst can say, *"It was not implemented properly."* This approach is copied from economists and allows one to sound authoritative without doing any research and without committing either way.

I was very surprised that none of the analysis on two-tiered ERP brought up the fact that the analysis was contradictory to the original logic of ERP, something that I consider to be one of the biggest stories related to two-tiered ERP. Another letdown was that not a single IT analyst asked the question: If two-tiered ERP is so advantageous and saves so much money, what does this mean regarding Tier 1 ERP?

An Algorithm for Starting Trends Without Evidence

This is how trends get started in enterprise software; the process seems to have the following stages:

1. *The Marketing Machine:* Software vendors with a financial bias propose something is a good idea and rev up the marketing machine.

2. *Stoking the Fire:* IT analysts write reports on the idea, without declaring the source of the new idea—the financially biased software vendors. They do

not evaluate the merits of the proposal, but instead write articles—perhaps with a few anecdotes of why "it could be" a good idea.

3. *The Conference Circuit:* Vendors and consultants start presenting on the topic at conferences, and articles are written about the idea in IT publications.

4. *The Conference Aftermath:* Purchasing company executives attend these conferences, and come back saying, *"We need to take a look at two-tiered ERP."*

5. *The Surveys:* Surveys are performed that show that X percent of executives are thinking about whether or not to implement the new idea.

Enterprise software buyers are thus primed for the marketing materials and sales pitches from the software vendors that **started the trend** in the first place. This is very reminiscent of how topics become popular in national politics. Often an event will occur, prompting a number of stories on the topic. Then a survey is taken and the survey shows that this topic (not without coincidence) is on people's minds.

Another person was able to control public opinion in the same manner. His name was William Randolph Hearst and here is his famous cable:

> *"When Hearst Artist Frederic Remington, cabled from Cuba in 1897 that 'there will be no war,' William Randolph Hearst cabled back: 'You furnish the pictures and I'll furnish the war.'"*

The above essentially describes how historically media outlets have been used to manipulate what people think and what they feel. The history of media in general goes back much further than the history of media for enterprise software. In fact, the history of enterprise software only goes back to roughly 1970 (most software applications prior to this period were shrouded in secrecy as they were military in nature). However, many of the same outcomes are consistent to the point of repetitiveness, and are easy to catch if one studies the topic. Knowledgeable entities can influence media systems. In fact, a major impetus of marketing is to influence storylines in a way that makes them seem entirely authentic.[24]

Conclusion

SAP and Oracle have attempted to control the two tier ERP story and to co-opt the trend so that their customers buy lower tier ERP systems from them. Neither of these software vendors have proven to provide good information to their customers, and, in fact, both gouge their customers to a ridiculous degree on support costs. They should have zero credibility with buyers, especially if one actually evaluates their history of being right with their previous predictions and advice. Of course the bad quality information on this topic is not limited to SAP and Oracle. This chapter provided numerous examples of evidence free statements made by those that often have a substantial influence on the information technology media and also what buyers think.

---

[24] How conventional wisdom is controlled by entities with major "pull" is one of the great undercover stories of enterprise software. Evidence-free statements are often couched in terms related to "what clients want," when, in fact, it is the proposers themselves who have that opinion. A good example of this can be found in the following quotation.

> "'Customers have been telling us that delivery options in certain areas make sense for isolated business processes where small sales units want a rapid start and can get going quickly,' SAP's Wohl said. 'Complex business processes that run across the business are considered strategic and critical and customers say they just don't want to lose control.' Similarly, former SAP technology leader Shai Agassi said that companies would not be willing to put core business processes on the Internet and that software as a service would not affect core operating processes."

Isn't it coincidental that SAP's customers are telling them exactly what is in line with SAP's business interests? (SAP is weak in SaaS and strong in on-premises.) Secondly, SAP spends a great deal of time telling customers not to move "core" and "complex" business processes away from on-premises, so who is telling who this narrative? I am not the only person to see the self-centered statements made by SAP representatives, as the following quotation attests.

> "Our thoughtful response to these well-prepared statements is BUNK! To say that ERP data is more critical than CRM data is ridiculous. For most organizations, their two most valuable information assets are their customer list and their sales information—data contained in CRM applications. To imply that sales processes are less 'complex' and strategic than entering accounting transactions into an ERP system is completely without merit. We suggest that Mr. Wohl cease trying to protect his on-premise turf and truly harvest the opportunity to apply SAP's back office ERP domain knowledge toward an on-demand ERP application which compliments an on-demand CRM solution." — Online CRM

CHAPTER 6

Applying the Concept of Two-tiered ERP to Your Company

The basic proposal that two-tiered ERP reduces costs **can be true**. According to research that is available at Software Decisions, the cost savings on the basis of total costs of ownership (TCO) can range from the a slightly negative cost savings (that is a cost increase) to roughly **one fourth of costs** when compared to the TCO of providing ERP functionality for users with a 100 percent tier 1 ERP stategy. However, it is not possible to ascribe a specific value to the cost savings estimate without knowing the following:

1. The specific ERP systems to be used

2. How many ERP systems are in the mix

3. How many instances are to be modeled

This is because the savings entirely depend upon factors such as the following:

1. *ERP TCO Variability:* ERP applications have a high variability in their total cost of ownership. There is also a weak relationship

between the cost of the ERP system and its capabilities—meaning some of the best ERP systems are the least expensive—but also most often not included in a software selection as they lack the brand name, marketing and coverage of IT analysts and recommendations of consulting companies.

2. *Degree of Transition to the Tier 2 ERP Application(s):* The more users are transitioned to the Tier 2 ERP application, **the more money will be saved**. If a company has a thousand total users and transitions seven hundred of them to a tier 2 ERP application, the predicted savings will be higher than if the same company were to transition only five hundred users to a tier 2 ERP application.

Of course, reduced costs are not the only benefits of two tier ERP strategy—one of the major benefits is having more diversity of functionality, and a better fit between the application and the business requirements. Too often this is lost in the story of cost reduction brought by two tier ERP. However, it bears emphasizing that following a two tier ERP strategy **can** lead to lower costs, but it is not automatic. It very much depends upon how the strategy is implemented. The benefits come down to the quality of the software selection and the depth of the analysis regarding the overall solution architecture of ERP systems. Something that is also open to debate is how the ERP systems would be integrated. I have already stated that the commonly presented practice of integrating ERP systems to one another is less cost effective than integrating all the ERP systems to a common or master BI system. Therefore, chosing to follow a two tier ERP strategy is **really just the starting point** of a series of questions, each of which must be carefully analyzed and effectively decided. If errors are made along the way, it is actually exceedingly easy to end up with a two tier implementation that nets the company little benefit. Proponents present two tier ERP oversimplify the actual outcomes of following the strategy as if those that follow it essentially can't lose.

Proponents of two-tiered ERP are correct when they state that the strategy can save companies money. However, in addition to exaggering the cost savings, they are trying to have their cake and eat it too by proposing cost savings without explaining the **actual reasons** for the cost savings. Some of the proponents of two tiered ERP are silent on the underlying reason for the cost savings for political reasons. They want to sell their ERP software, but don't want to offend their propects who have sizable investments, often poorly performing investments into tier 1 ERP applications. Another reason that proponents don't want to explain the underlying reason is that they do not want to offend their supporters, which is the case with NetSuite—which will bring up how much a two tiered ERP strategy can save SAP customers, but is mum on how much it can save Oracle customers—because of their business relationship with Oracle.

Additionally, two tier ERP proponents have a strong tendency to leave out the history of ERP in an effort to keep their audience focused on their final conclusion, a final conclusion that is an oversimplification of what we know about ERP systems. This serves to provide a misimpression as to important features of a two-tiered ERP strategy. These misimpressions are listed below:

1. *The Novelty of Two-Tiered ERP:* Two-tiered ERP is not new. Most companies that use ERP already use different ERP applications for their various tiers.

2. *The Reason for the Cost Savings of Two-Tiered ERP:* Many of the proponents of two-tiered ERP are quick to point out the cost savings that come from following the strategy, but are relatively silent on why this should be the case. The reason is very simple: **Tier 1 ERP systems are expensive and furthermore do not provide companies with much of a return on investment** (actually our research at Software Decisions concludes that most tier 1 ERP systems have a **negative** return on investment). That is, most companies would have been better off both financially and operationally if they had never purchased or implemented their tier 1 ERP system. Two-tiered ERP is often presented as if it is some great innovative idea, when, in fact, an inefficient system is simply being replaced with slightly more efficient systems. Here's an analogy. Let's say a wealthy family purchased five Lamborghinis. A family friend points out that if they sold four of the Lamborghinis (keep one Lamborghini for social appearances) and instead bought four Hondas, the family's automotive costs would decline by following a "two-tiered automobile strategy." Quite naturally, a Lamborghini is a hugely expensive prestige item. It should not be considered some great intellectual breakthrough that one can reduce one's automotive budget by replacing Lamborghinis with more practical automobiles. If the tier 1 systems are so cost inefficient a good question that many companies should

consider asking themselves is who recommended purchasing the tier 1 ERP systems in the first place?

Two-tiered ERP will save companies money. Most proponents of two-tiered ERP would like the recipients of their message to stop the analysis at that point, and to simply buy a Tier 2 ERP system (from them) and have that be the end of the discussion. However, it should definitely not be the end of the discussion. At Software Decisions, a comparison of multiple solution architecture strategies were performed, which are available at this link:

http://www.scmfocus.com/softwaredecisions/plans/solution-architecture-packages/

The findings are that, while two-tiered ERP is a cost savings strategy, it is not the strategy that **saves companies the most money** or provides the most functionality or the lowest long term maintenance. ERP companies and consulting companies that are signed up to the two tiered approach can't tell you what is the best overall strategy—because they have a particular offering to sell.

The strategy that does is a best-of-breed strategy that uses a best-of-breed application in every area, including a best-of-breed financial and accounting system. This strategy may also use an ERP system, but the highest-rated ERP systems are not the most well-known ERP systems; rather they are lesser known systems that provide much better value, and unlike the Tier 1 ERP applications and many of the Tier 2 ERP applications, the best-of-breed vendors "play nice" with other applications rather than using the ERP sale as a wedge to force in more applications (a strategy that is referred to as "penetrate and radiate"). Instead, the best ERP software values in the market come from specialized vendors who only provide ERP software—not from software conglomerates whose ERP applications are simply one of their many offerings and who are planning their next acquisition.

The best-of-breed strategy has the extra benefit of providing the **best total functionality**. Research available at Software Decisions clearly shows that companies that follow this strategy will **save between roughly one-third and one-half** on their overall solution architecture TCO, and this is **including all integration costs**. This compares to a predicted cost savings of between an actual cost increase and one-quarter for a two-tiered ERP strategy. Furthermore, the best-of-breed strategy combines the largest possible cost savings with the best functionality of any other strategy, meaning it also provides the highest predicted return on investment. Two-tiered ERP does provide some additional variability in functionality, but the benefits are primarily on the cost side of the equation. Therefore, moving to a two-tiered strategy is an improvement over deploying single instance ERP, but it is **not** the best strategy that a company can follow.

Implementing the Two Tiered ERP Strategy

Therefore, for companies looking for the best overall solution architecture strategy, it's neither employing a 100 percent tier 1 ERP strategy, nor a two-teired ERP strategy (both of which would be augmented with what is often mediocre applications offered by the ERP vendor for "integration" along with other assorted best of breed applications.

However, executive decision makers most often don't have the authority to review the overall corporate solution architecture, but instead must make decisions on incremental additions to their corporate solution architecture. For these decision makers, a the first question with respect to two tiered ERP is whether it is better than 100 percent tier 1 ERP strategy, and for this the answer is yes. The second question is *"which tier 2 ERP system,"* and final question is *"what is the best way to integrate all of the ERP systems."* The answer to the first question is that it very much depends upon how the two tier strategy is implemented, as has already been discussed in this chapter. Now we will look at the second of these two questions.

Choosing a Two Tier ERP System

Many ERP software vendors present themselves to their prospects as if they have the best answer for how to choose a two tier ERP system, and the answer is unsurprisingly **their software**. ERP vendors have made the case that some ERP vendors have a leg up on others in terms of being the tier 2 or tier 3 ERP application. After analyzing this area, as well as their documentation and their statements, it's difficult to see how any of this argument holds any water. The best reason not to believe something is if it has no evidence, but in this case there are two other reasons why it's not a good idea to listen to ERP vendors on the topic of two tier ERP.

1. *Solution Architecture Role*: ERP vendors are attempting to serve as solution architects for their clients when they propose why their software is part of a grand two tier ERP strategy. There is a long history of software vendors and consulting companies serving as solution architects for buyers, and it rarely works out well. Software vendors cannot look after the overall architecture because of their bias to insert their applications at every turn.

2. *Distraction*: The advantages of a two tier ERP strategy are based upon a buyer gaining access to a lower cost and lower maintenance ERP system, **it is not** based upon integration. It is **worth repeating** this because many ERP vendors are combining several issues which will always lead to confusion on the part of buyers. The primary benefit of two tiered ERP is based upon getting access to a lower cost and lower maintenance ERP system as well as gaining access to more functionality, which can meet more business requirements without expensive customization. Let us remember, that if the main objective were an integrated system, and if one integrated system lead to lower costs, then we would simply stick with a 100 percent tier 1 ERP strategy. However, companies that have followed this strategy have experienced the highest possible costs of **any possible ERP solution architecture**. And in this vein, the most beneficial ERP system is the one that best meets the business requirements of the company.

Many ERP vendors are proposing the old integration argument, and the Tier 2 and Tier 3 ERP vendors will discuss how their systems integrate better to the teir 2 ERP system that is already in place. However, a tier 2 ERP strategy can be implemented with the ERP system—but this is not the way to implement this strategy—which leads into the final question.

How to Integrate the Tier 2 or Tier 3 ERP System
ERP systems must be integrated to other ERP systems for really two reasons—one is the two entities that run each ERP system do business with each other, and

therefore it may be convenient if the two ERP systems are integrated—however it's certainly a minor consideration. Unrelated companies have no problem doing business with each other when their ERP systems are not integrated through the standard business documents/transactions of purchase orders, sales orders, etc. Secondly, ERP systems were never designed to be integrated to other ERP systems. The second, and far more important reason for ERP systems that are within the same overall enterprise to be integrated, is reporting. However, ERP systems are not generally all that proficient at reporting—which is the primary capability of business intelligence systems. ERP systems can have data extracted from them and sent to business intelligence systems, and two or more ERP systems can be integrated to a single business intelligence system in the same way. In fact, this is the most logical way of implementing multiple ERP systems that result in integrated reporting. The fact that a company already uses one particular BI application should **not** promote that company to try to purchase an ERP system from the same vendor. This is because getting the best ERP system and best business intelligence system for the company's requirements is far **more** important than getting the systems with some faux integration that comes from the same vendor. Just the analysis of long term maintenance costs between the different ERP applications demonstrates this, but of course the other side of the story is the functionality differences between the ERP applications that are often quite significant. For example, in the case of ProcessPro, an ERP system that is customized for process industry manufacturing (things like cheese, petroleum refining, mining, etc.) the applications come standard with a number of key areas of functionality that no other ERP system have in total, but many other ERP vendors partially have or pretend to have. Process industry manufacturing buyers that choose systems that have less of this specialized functionality, accepting the integration argument, or that the customization will be "not that big of a deal," end up with problematic ERP implementations that cost a lot to maintain. Hopefully, this emphasizes the importance of mating the application to the requirements—although there are many other examples that could be given. Furthermore, there is no software vendor that offers both a leading ERP system and a leading business intelligence system. In fact, the software vendors that offer ERP systems offer some of the lowest productivity and highest cost business intelligence systems, and purchasing both from one vendor is a guarantee of ending up with at least one bad application.[25]

Conclusion

In order to implement two-tier 2 strategy most effectively, it's necessary to resist the arguments presented by two tier ERP proponents and also to dig a little deeper into **under what circumstaces and why** following a two tier ERP strategy can save companies money. Many proponents of two tier ERP will make the argument that their systems are better suited to be the second or third tier, when in fact any ERP system can be equally placed in these tiers. The hyperbole on two tiered ERP should not distract buyers from attempting to find the best match between the ERP system and the business requirements. Secondly, it is in most cases unnecessary to integrate the multiple ERP systems that are part of a multi-tiered ERP solution architecture. Even when companies buy and sell from one another, all of this can, and is, easily managed with standard purchase order and sales order functionality that requires no integration. For consolidated reporting it is necessary to have all of the ERP systems in the company's ecosystem to have data extracted from them, but again, here the most important feature is the capabilities and the productivity of the business intelligence solution. The best software vendors in business intelligence do not offer ERP systems, but some of the lower quality and higher cost ERP vendors do. The best approach is to find the **highest value** applications in both ERP and business intelligence and combine them as on any other project, there are simply no "special rules" when it comes to two tiered ERP.

---

[25] The research supporting this statement is too detailed to include in the book. However, it is part of the Software Selection Package for Big ERP, and the Software Selection Package for BI at Software Decisions, which can be seen at this link: http://www.scmfocus.com/softwaredecisions/plans/solution-architecture-packages/.

CHAPTER 7

Conclusion

The term two tier ERP means applying different ERP systems to different "tiers" of the business. In a nutshell, the larger and more prominent parent companies tend to receive the tier 1 applications, while the subsidiaries receive ERP systems that are considered tier 2. IT analysts and software vendors present a model where multiple ERP systems are connected to a master ERP system. However, there is no real evidence provided as to why this is a good thing, and it is also contradictory to the design of ERP systems, as ERP systems are designed to represent the "enterprise," and not to be connected to other ERP systems. Furthermore, attempting to integrate multiple ERP systems increases the expense of following a multi-ERP system strategy.

Two tier ERP is a repudiation of the concept of a "single instance ERP," and shows that this powerful concept, which drove IT decision making for so long is finally beginning to give way to the reality that a diversity of applications—both ERP and non ERP, are required in order to meet business requirements. In fact, two tier ERP can be considered one of the first cracks in the façade of tier 1 ERP systems, something that, if enterprise software decisions were primarily based upon research and historical analysis, rather than based upon trends and "what other people are doing," would have occurred some time ago.

To many, two tier ERP comes across as a thoughtful enterprise software strategy. Hhowever, an analysis of the origins of two tier ERP point to it being nothing more than a marketing construct that was first proposed, or at least popularized by NetSuite. Marketing constructs can be true or false, but it's important to identify the source of any concept in order to understand why it was proposed in the first place. This is not done in the IT press, nor has it been done in any other writing that I read as part of the literature for this book.

The two tier ERP construct was designed to open up the clients that were primarily tier 1 ERP customers to tier two and three ERP products. There is really nothing more than anecdotal evidence quoted that is used to demonstrate that two tier ERP systems reduces costs/provide benefits over a 100 percent tier 1 strategy. Given the high expense and low value of tier 1 ERP systems, it would be surprising if a two tier strategy, if properly configured, **did not** improve outcomes for buyers. However, depending upon the scenario, it is in fact quite possible for a two tier ERP strategy to be more expensive than a 100 percent tier 1 ERP strategy.

SAP and Oracle have attempted to control the two tier ERP story and to co-opt the trend so that their customers buy lower tier ERP systems from them. Neither of these software vendors have proven to provide good information to their customers, and, in fact, both gouge their customers to a ridiculous degree on support costs. They should have low credibility with buyers, especially if one actually evaluates their history of being right with their previous predictions and advice. Of course the poor quality information on this topic is not limited to SAP and Oracle, and this brings up the point of how important it is to check the track records of those that would provide "advice" as to which way to go on two tier ERP.

Two tier ERP proponents are providing an overly simplistic and somewhat misleading explanation of what makes the strategy work. They are also deliberately overstating the expected cost savings from the strategy and overgeneralizing how frequently these savings can be expected. The cost savings entirely depends upon how the two tier ERP strategy is employed. Research available at Software Decisions shows a wide variability in cost savings depending upon factors such as how many users are transitioned to the non-tier 1 ERP system, on which ERP systems are part of the strategy—and these are just a few of the variables that must be considered.

Strangely, proponents of two tier ERP do not tend to focus on the benefits of receiving a broader range of functionality, which can better meet business requirements—which is **another important** benefit of two tier ERP. However diversity in applications works not only for ERP systems, but also for other software categories, and this relates to another factor that is left out by two tier ERP proponents, and this is that two tier ERP **is not** actually the best or lowest cost IT strategy. This omission is not surprising as the strongest two tier ERP strategy proponents are non tier 1 ERP vendors. Research available at Software Decisions shows that a best of breed strategy saves significantly more money on the basis of total cost of ownership than moving to a two tier ERP strategy, and also results in better functionality. This book should make clear that proposals by proponents of two tier ERP must not be taken at face value, but should be carefully analyzed and fact checked. Not performing the necessary research and relying upon information sources with serious financial bias is what lead to so many buyers ending up with such low performing ERP systems in the first place. It's important not to repeat those mistakes with two tier ERP.

About Software Decisions

The overall story of the cost benefits of moving toward two-tiered ERP is extremely interesting and compelling. To clarify the cost benefits, Software Decisions developed a self-service comparison tool that allows anyone to determine the combined cost of multiple ERP systems within a company—and to compare a single Tier 1 ERP strategy to a two-tiered ERP strategy. This is a fee-based analysis, but for those interested in the comparison of each strategy on the basis of total cost of ownership, the analysis will prove quite informative and may allow for better decision making. This analysis can be viewed at the following link:

http://www.softwaredecisions.org

Other Books from SCM Focus

Bill of Materials in Excel, ERP, Planning and PLM/BMMS Software

http://www.scmfocus.com/scmfocuspress/the-software-approaches-for-improving-your-bill-of-materials-book/

Constrained Supply and Production Planning in SAP APO

http://www.scmfocus.com/scmfocuspress/select-a-book/constrained-supply-and-production-planning-in-sap-apo/

Enterprise Software Risk: Controlling the Main Risk Factors on IT Projects

http://www.scmfocus.com/scmfocuspress/it-decision-making-books/enterprise-software-project-risk-management/

Enterprise Software Selection: How to Pinpoint the Perfect Software Solution using Multiple Information Sources

http://www.scmfocus.com/scmfocuspress/it-decision-making-books/entcrprise-software-selection/

Enterprise Software TCO: Calculating and Using Total Cost of Ownership for Decision Making

http://www.scmfocus.com/scmfocuspress/it-decision-making-books/enterprise-software-tco/

Gartner and the Magic Quadrant: A Guide for Buyers, Vendors and Investors

http://www.scmfocus.com/scmfocuspress/it-decision-making-books/gartner-and-the-magic-quadrant/

Inventory Optimization and Multi-Echelon Planning Software

http://www.scmfocus.com/scmfocuspress/supply-books/the-inventory-optimization-and-multi-echelon-software-book/

Multi-Method Supply Planning in SAP APO

http://www.scmfocus.com/scmfocuspress/select-a-book/multi-method-supply-planning-in-sap-apo/

Planning Horizons, Calendars and Timings in SAP APO

http://www.scmfocus.com/scmfocuspress/select-a-book/planning-horizons-calendars-and-timings-in-sap-apo/

Process Industry Manufacturing Software: ERP, Planning, Recipe, MES & Process Control

http://www.scmfocus.com/scmfocuspress/production-books/process-industry-planning/

Replacing Big ERP: Breaking the Big ERP Habit with Best of Breed Applications at a Fraction of the Cost

http://www.scmfocus.com/scmfocuspress/erp-books/replacing-erp/

Setting Up the Supply Network in SAP APO

http://www.scmfocus.com/scmfocuspress/select-a-book/setting-up-the-supply-network-in-sap-apo/

SuperPlant: Creating a Nimble Manufacturing Enterprise with Adaptive Planning Software

http://www.scmfocus.com/scmfocuspress/production-books/the-superplant-concept/

Supply Chain Forecasting Software

http://www.scmfocus.com/scmfocuspress/the-statistical-and-consensus-supply-chain-forecasting-software-book/

Supply Planning with MRP, DRP and APS Software

http://www.scmfocus.com/scmfocuspress/supply-books/the-supply-planning-with-mrpdrp-and-aps-software-book/

The Real Story Behind ERP: Separating Fact from Fiction

http://www.scmfocus.com/scmfocuspress/erp-books/the-real-story-behind-erp/

Spreading the Word

SCM Focus Press is a small publisher. However, we pride ourselves on publishing the unvarnished truth that most other publishers will not publish. If you felt like you learned something valuable from reading this book, please spread the word by adding a review to our page on Amazon.com.

Author Profile

Shaun Snapp is the Founder and Editor of SCM Focus. SCM Focus is one of the largest independent supply chain software analysis and educational sites on the Internet.

After working at several of the largest consulting companies and at i2 Technologies, he became an independent consultant and later started SCM Focus. He maintains a strong interest in comparative software design, and works both in SAP APO, as well as with a variety of best-of-breed supply chain planning vendors. His ongoing relationships with these vendors keep him on the cutting edge of emerging technology.

Primary Sources of Information and Writing Topics

Shaun writes about topics with which he has first-hand experience. These topics range from recovering problematic implementations, to system configuration, to socializing complex software and supply chain concepts in the areas of demand planning, supply planning and production planning.

More broadly, he writes on topics supportive of these applications, which include master data parameter management, integration, analytics, simulation and bill of material management systems. He covers management aspects of enterprise software ranging from software policy to handling consulting partners on SAP projects.

Shaun writes from an implementer's perspective and as a result he focuses on how software is actually used in practice rather than its hypothetical or "pure release note capabilities." Unlike many authors in enterprise software who keep their distance from discussing the realities of software implementation, he writes both on the problems as well as the successes of his software use. This gives him a distinctive voice in the field.

Secondary Sources of Information
In addition to project experience, Shaun's interest in academic literature is a secondary source of information for his books and articles. Intrigued with the historical perspective of supply chain software, much of his writing is influenced by his readings and research into how different categories of supply chain software developed, evolved, and finally became broadly used over time.

Covering the Latest Software Developments
Shaun is focused on supply chain software selections and implementation improvement through writing and consulting, bringing companies some of the newest technologies and methods. Some of the software developments that Shaun showcases at SCM Focus and in books at SCM Focus Press have yet to reach widespread adoption.

Education
Shaun has an undergraduate degree in business from the University of Hawaii, a Masters of Science in Maritime Management from the Maine Maritime Academy and a Masters of Science in Business Logistics from Penn State University. He has taught both logistics and SAP software.

Software Certifications

Shaun has been trained and/or certified in applications from i2 Technologies, Servigistics, ToolsGroup and SAP (SD, DP, SNP, SPP, EWM).

Contact

Shaun can be contacted at: shaunsnapp@scmfocus.com or www.scmfocus.com/

Links in the Book

Chapter 1

http://www.scmfocus.com/writing-rules/

http://www.scmfocus.com

http://www.scmfocus.com/scmfocuspress/erp-books/the-real-story-
behind-two-tier-erp/

Chapter 3

http://www.scmfocus.com/sapprojectmanagement/2010/07/sap-will-
never-support-soa/

http://www.softwaredecisions.org

http://www.scmfocus.com/softwaredecisions/plans/solution-
architecture-packages/

Chapter 4

http://www.scmfocus.com/inventoryoptimizationmultiechelon/
2010/01/its-time-for-the-sap-xapps-program-to-die/

http://www.scmfocus.com/enterprisesoftwarepolicy/2012/01/27/how-
common-is-it-for-sap-to-take-intellectual-property-from-partners/

Chapter 5

http://www.scmfocus.com/softwaredecisions/plans/solution-architecture-packages/

http://www.netsuite.com/portal/landing/accenture.shtml

http://www.oracle.com/us/corporate/press/1966087

http://www.scmfocus.com/sapintegration/2011/11/15/what-are-saps-vendor-integration-certifications-worth-on-projects/

Chapter 6

http://www.scmfocus.com/softwaredecisions/plans/solution-architecture-packages/

http://www.softwaredecisions.org

http://www.scmfocus.com/softwaredecisions/plans/solution-architecture-packages/

Chapter 7

http://www.softwaredecisions.org

Abbreviations

CRM: Customer Relationship Management

DRP: Distribution Resource Planning

ECSS: Expeditionary Combat Support System

EDI: Electronic Data Interchange

ERP: Enterprise Resource Planning

MRP: Material Requirements Planning

ROA: Return on Assets

ROI: Return on Investment

ROS: Return on Sales

SaaS: Software as a Service

SCM: Supply Chain Management

TCO: Total Cost of Ownership

References

Aghazadeh, Seyed-Mahmoud. *MRP Contributes to a Company's Profitability.* 2003.

Al-Mashari, Majed. Al-Mudimigh, Abdulla. Ziari, Mohamed. *Enterprise Resource Planning: A Taxonomy of Critical Factors.* European Journal of Operations Research, June 2002.

Angell, Marcia. *The Truth About the Drug Companies.* July 15, 2004. http://www.wanttoknow.info/truthaboutdrugcompanies.

Antidepressant Medications Are Ineffective and Misleading. http://truthindrugs.com/pdf/ads.pdf.

Baase, Sara. *IBM: Producer or Predator.* April 1974. http://www-rohan.sdsu.edu/faculty/giftfire/ibm.html.

Bardach, Eugene. *A Practical Guide for Policy Analysis: The Eightfold Path to More Effective Problem Solving (4th Edition).* CQ Press: College Publishing Group, 2011.

Bartholomew, Doug. *Realizing ERP's Untapped Potential. Pharmaceutical Manufacturing.* September 7, 2005. http://www.pharmamanufacturing.com/articles/2004/242/.

Bezruchka, Stephen. *The Hurrider I Go, The Behinder I Get: The Deteriorating International Ranking of U.S. Health Status.* January 3, 2012.
http://www.annualreviews.org/doi/pdf/10.1146/annurev-publhealth-031811-124649.

Biello, David. *Grass Makes Better Ethanol than Corn Does*. Scientific American. January 8, 2008. http://www.scientificamerican.com/article.cfm?id=grass-makes-better-ethanol-than-corn.

Birch, Nicholas. *Why ERP Doesn't Work*. June 2007. http://www.istart.co.nz/index/HM20/PC0/PVC197/EX27129/AR29697.

Bridgwater, Adrian. *ERP is Dead, Long Live Two-Tier ERP*. December 12, 2012. http://www.computerweekly.com/blogs/cwdn/2012/12/erp-is-dead-long-live-two-tier-erp.html.

Burns, Michael. *What Does an ERP System Cost?* CA Magazine. August 2011. http://www.camagazine.com/archives/print-edition/2011/aug/columns/camagazine50480.aspx.

Castenllina, Nick. *To ERP or Not to ERP: In Manufacturing, It Isn't Even a Question*. March 31, 2011. http://aberdeen.com/aberdeen-library/7116/RA-enterprise-resource-planning.aspx.

Chen, Injazz J. *Planning for ERP Systems: Analysis and Future Trend*. Business Process Management Journal, 2001.

Chiappinelli, Chris. *New ERP Paradigm Challenges Old Assumptions*. March 2, 2011. www.techmatchpro.com/article/2011/3/new-erp-paradigm-challenges-old-assumptions.

Clarke, Gavin. *Larry 'Shared Databases are Crap' Ellison Reveals Shared Oracle Database*. October 1, 2012. http://www.theregister.co.uk/2012/10/01/ellison_oow_2012_database_cloud/.

Columbus, Louis. *ERP Prediction for 2013: The Customer Takes Control*. Forbes, January 7, 2013. http://www.forbes.com/sites/louiscolumbus/2013/01/07/erp-prediction-for-2013-the-customer-takes-control/.

Corn Ethanol. Accessed July 3, 2013. http://en.wikipedia.org/wiki/Corn_ethanol.

Elragal, Ahmed and Al-Serafi, Ayman. *The Effect of ERP System Implementation on Business Performance: An Exploratory Case-Study*. June 2011. http://www.ibimapublishing.com/journals/CIBIMA/2011/670212/670212.pdf.

Enterprise Resource Planning. Accessed July 23, 2013. http://en.wikipedia.org/wiki/Enterprise_resource_planning.

ERP: Is High ROI with Low TCO Possible? Aberdeen Group, 2012.

Fear, Uncertainty and Doubt. Accessed August 25, 2013.
    http://en.wikipedia.org/wiki/Fear,_uncertainty_and_doubt.

Hall, Susan. *Third-Party ERP Support: When It Makes Sense.* October 4, 2012.
    http://www.enterpriseappstoday.com/erp/third-party-erp-support-when-it-makes-
    sense.html.

Hawthorne Effect. Accessed July 16, 2013.
    http://en.wikipedia.org/wiki/Hawthorne_effect.

Henry Ford. Last modified November 6, 2013.
    http://en.wikipedia.org/wiki/Henry_Ford.

History of IBM. Accessed July 26, 2013.
    http://en.wikipedia.org/wiki/History_of_IBM.

Information Technology and Cloud Services: Why Big Systems are Here to Stay
    http://www.accenture.com/SiteCollectionDocuments/Podcast/Accenture-IT-Cloud-
    Podcast-Transcript.pdf

Insel, Thomas. *Directors Blog: Antidepressants: A Complicated Picture.* December 6,
    2011.
    http://www.nimh.nih.gov/about/director/2011/antidepressants-a-complicated-
    picture.shtml.

Jurtras, Mint. *The High Cost of Business Disruption in Modifying and Maintaining
    ERP,* 2013.

Kahan, Dan, Peters, Ellen, Dawson, Erica and Slovic, Paul. *Motivated Numeracy and
    Enlightened Self-Government.* September 3, 2013.
    http://papers.ssrn.com/sol3/papers.cfm?abstract_id=2319992.

Kanaracus, Chris. *Air Force Scraps Massive ERP Project After Racking Up $1 Billion
    in Cost.* November 14, 2012.
    http://www.cio.com/article/721628/Air_Force_scraps_massive_ERP_project_after_
    racking_up_1_billion_in_costs.

Kimberling, Eric. *Are Two-Tier ERP Systems Finally Becoming Mainstream?*
    December 19, 2012.
    http://panorama-consulting.com/are-two-tier-erp-systems-finally-becoming-
    mainstream/.

Lawrie, George. *It's Time To Clarify Your Global ERP Strategy.* Forrester.
    December 9 2010.

Legacy System. Accessed October 28, 2013.
   http://en.wikipedia.org/wiki/Legacy_system.

List of Countries by Total Health Expenditure Per Capita. September 1, 2013.
   http://en.wikipedia.org/wiki/List_of_countries_by_total_health_expenditure_
   (PPP)_per_capita.

List of Largest Companies by Revenue. Last modified November 16, 2013.
   http://en.wikipedia.org/wiki/List_of_largest_companies_by_revenue.

Logical Fallacies. Accessed October 28, 2013.
   http://en.wikipedia.org/wiki/List_of_fallacies.

Lovett, Jeff. Duning, Tim. McDonnell, Monica. *Accelerating the Value of ERP
   Conversion Projects.* Teradata. 2012.

Mallory, James. *ERP Budget & Cost Considerations: Moving from QuickBooks to ERP.*
   http://blog.e2benterprise.com/erp-budget-cost-considerations-moving-from-
   quickbooks-to-erp-part-5-of-8-part-series/.

Mann, Charles. *Why Software Is Bad.* Technology Review. July 1, 2002.
   http://www.technologyreview.com/featuredstory/401594/why-software-is-so-bad/.

Mar, Anna. *12 Mind Bending ERP Statistics.* September 11, 2011.
   http://simplicable.com/new/12-mind-bending-ERP-statistics.

Markus, M. Lynne. *Enterprise Resource Planning: Multisite ERP Implementations.
   Association for Computing Machinery.* April 1, 2000.

Montgomery, Nigel. Ganly, Denise. *How to Determine If a Two-Tier ERP Suite
   Strategy Is Right for You.* Gartner. 24 October 2012.

Montgomery, Nigel. *Understand the Deployment Options for a Two-Tier ERP Suite
   Strategy.* Gartner. 15 May 2013.

Moon, Andy. *Are the Rewards of ERP Systems Worth the Risk.* March 27, 2008.
   http://www.techrepublic.com/blog/it-news-digest/are-the-rewards-of-erp-systems-
   worth-the-risk/.

Murry, Christopher. *Ranking 37th: Measuring the Performance of the U.S. Health
   Care System.* January 14, 2010.
   http://www.nejm.org/doi/full/10.1056/NEJMp0910064.

Nystrom, Christiana and Windler, Maria. *ERP System and Effects: A Comparison of
   Theory and Practice.* Gotenborg University, 2003.

Olsen, Art. *ERP: Repair or Replace.* April 1, 2013.
   http://www.pcbennettconsulting.com/erp-repair-or-replace/.

Opportunity Cost. Accessed June 22, 2013.
  https://en.wikipedia.org/wiki/Opportunity_cost.

Pabo-Nazao, Placid and Raymond, Louis *In House Development as an Alternative for ERP Adoption by SMES: A Critical Case Study,* 2009.

Perera, David. *Air Force Considering Alternatives to Key ERP.* October 30, 2011.
  http://www.fiercegovernmentit.com/story/air-force-considering-alternatives-key-erp/2011-10-30.

Philips, Steven Scott. *Control Your ERP Destiny: Reduce Project Costs, Mitigate Risks, and Design Better Business Solutions.* Street Smart ERP Publications, 2012.

Process Industry ERP Requirements. Wonderware, 2000.

Propaganda. October 28, 2013.
  http://en.wikipedia.org/wiki/Propaganda.

Prouty, Kevin and Castellina, Nick. *To ERP or Not to ERP.* April 2011.
  http://www.plex.com/wordpress/wp-content/uploads/2012/05/Aberdeen-ERPvsNoERP.pdf.

Proving a Negative. Accessed March 15, 2013.
  http://en.wikipedia.org/wiki/Proving_a_negative.

Radding, Alan. *ERP: More Than an Application.* Information Week, 1999.

Rettig, Cynthia. *The Trouble With Enterprise Software.* MIT Sloan, Fall 2007.
  http://sloanreview.mit.edu/article/the-trouble-with-enterprise-software/.

Rich, Michael. *Standards for High-Quality Research and Analysis,* November 2011.
  http://www.rand.org/standards.html.

Rohm, Ted. *To ERP or Not to ERP, that Is the C-Level Question.* February 22, 2013.
  http://blog.technologyevaluation.com/blog/2013/02/22/to-erp-or-not-to-erp-that-is-the-c-level-question/.

Rokohl, Laura. *Visibility and Integration—The Key Ingredients for a Successful Supply Chain.* AspenTech. 2012.

Ross, J.W. *The ERP revolution: Surviving versus thriving.* MIT White Paper, November 1998.

Sabre (Computer System). Accessed July 16, 2013.
  http://en.wikipedia.org/wiki/Sabre_(computer_system).

Savitz, Eric. *The End of ERP.* February 9, 2012.
  http://www.forbes.com/sites/ciocentral/2012/02/09/the-end-of-erp/2/.

Singleton, Derek. *A Chronicle or ERP Software History Pt. II.* December 8, 2011. http://ctovision.com/2011/12/a-chronicle-of-erp-software-history-pt-ii/.

Slater, Derek and Koch, Christopher. *The ABCs of ERP.* http://paginas.fe.up.pt/~mgi00011/ERP/abcs_of_erp.htm.

Snapp, Shaun. *Enterprise Software Selection: How to Pinpoint the Perfect Software Solution Using Multiple Information Sources.* SCM Focus Press, 2013.

Snapp, Shaun. *Enterprise Software TCO: Calculating and Using Total Cost of Ownership for Decision Making.* SCM Focus Press, 2013.

Snapp, Shaun. *Gartner and the Magic Quadrant: A Guide for Buyers, Vendors, Investors.* SCM Focus Press, 2013.

Snapp, Shaun. *The Real Story Behind ERP: Separating Fact from Fiction.* SCM Focus Press, 2014.

Snapp, Shaun. *Process Industry Manufacturing Software: ERP, Planning, Recipe, MES & Process Control.* SCM Focus Press, 2013.

Snapp, Shaun. *Replacing Big ERP: Breaking the Big ERP Habit with Best-of-Breed Applications at a Fraction of the Cost.* SCM Focus Press, 2013.

Snapp, Shaun. *SuperPlant: Creating a Nimble Manufacturing Enterprise with Adaptive Planning Software.* SCM Focus Press. 2013.

Snapp, Shaun. *Supply Planning with MRP, DRP and APS Software.* SCM Focus Press, 2012.

Sommer, Brian. *ERP's Franken-soft and How Workday Avoids it.* November 13, 2012. http://www.zdnet.com/erps-franken-soft-and-how-workday-avoids-it-7000007200/.

SAP CRM Review. Online CRM. http://www.online-crm.com/sap.htm.

Stanley, George. *4 ERP Tips for FIAR Compliance,* 2013.

Stein, Tom. *Making ERP Add Up.* Information Week, 1999.

Stross, Randall. *Billion-Dollar Flop: Air Force Stumbles on Software Plan.* New York Times. December 8, 2012. http://www.nytimes.com/2012/12/09/technology/air-force-stumbles-over-software-modernization-project.html?_r=0.

Study Finds Antidepressants to be Depressingly Ineffective. August 2, 2012. http://www.globalhealingcenter.com/natural-health/study-finds-antidepressants-to-be-depressingly-ineffective/.

Tautology. Accessed June 27, 2013.
    http://en.wikipedia.org/wiki/Tautology_(rhetoric).

The Depressing News About Antidepressants. Newsweek. January 28, 2010.
    http://mag.newsweek.com/2010/01/28/the-depressing-news-about-
    antidepressants.html.

The Press: I'll Furnish the War. Time Magazine. 1947.
    http://content.time.com/time/magazine/article/0,9171,854840,00.html#ixzz2
    nmunytiC"

The Promise of ERP Systems. Enterprise Systems for Higher Education. Vol. 4, 2002.

Two-tier Enterprise Resource Planning. Accessed August 29, 2013.
    http://en.wikipedia.org/wiki/Enterprise_resource_planning#Two_tier_enterprise_
    resource_planning.

Wagner, David. *Old & Bad ERP All Over Manufacturing.* April 17, 2013.
    http://www.enterpriseefficiency.com/author.asp?section_id=1151&doc_id=262241.

Wailgum, Thomas. *ERP Sticker Shock: Maintenance, Upgrades and Customizations.*
    September 23, 2010.
    http://www.cio.com/article/618117/ERP_Sticker_Shock_Maintenance_Upgrades_
    and_Customizations.

Wailgum, Thomas. *SaaS ERP Has Buzz, But Who Are the Real Players?*
    March 10, 2010.
    http://www.cio.com/article/572463/SaaS_ERP_Has_Buzz_But_Who_Are_the_
    Real_Players.

Wailgum, Thomas. *Want to Save $10 Million or More on ERP? Don't Buy Oracle or
    SAP.* February 26, 2009.
    http://blogs.cio.com/thomas_wailgum/want_to_save_10_million_or_more_on_erp_
    dont_buy_oracle_or_sap?source=nlt_cioenterprise.

Wainewright, Phil. *ERP, RIP? Cloud Financials and Revenue Management in 2013.*
    January 4, 2013.
    http://www.zdnet.com/erp-rip-cloud-financials-and-revenue-management-in-2013-
    7000009376/.

Weill, Peter. *The Relationship Between Investment in Information Technology and
    Firm Performance: A Study of the Valve Manufacturing Sector.* December 1992.

What is ERP? NetSuite. August 27, 2001.
    http://www.netsuite.com/portal/resource/articles/erp/what-is-erp.shtml.

Why Implement a Two-tiered ERP Strategy. Sage.
http://na.sage.com/~/media/category/sna/assets/lp/sagebusinessknows/Documents/
resources/Sage_ERP_Two_Tier_Strategy.pdf

Wolpe, Toby. *When SAP Sprawl is Cool: Could Cutting Back your ERP be More Pain
than It's Worth?* May 9, 2013.
http://www.zdnet.com/are-businesses-wasting-millions-on-sap-erp-they-dont-
need-7000015133/.

Wood, Bill. *Overcome SAP-ERP System Integrator Sales Tactics.* May 9, 2011.
http://www.r3now.com/overcoming-sap-erp-system-integrator-sales-tactics-1/.

Worthen, Ben. *Extreme ERP Makeover.* December 9, 2003.
http://www.cio.com.au/article/181834/extreme_erp_makeover/?pp=5.

Year 2000 Problem. Accessed August 29, 2013.
http://en.wikipedia.org/wiki/Year_2000_problem.